BABYLONIAN

LITERATURE.

BABYLONIAN

LITERATURE:

LECTURES

DELIVERED AT THE ROYAL INSTITUTION.

BY THE

REV. A. H. SAYCE, M.A.

DEPUTY-PROFESSOR OF COMPARATIVE PHILOLOGY, OXFORD.

Author of "An Assyrian Grammar;" and "The Principles of Comparative Philology."

WIPF & STOCK · Eugene, Oregon

Wipf and Stock Publishers
199 W 8th Ave, Suite 3
Eugene, OR 97401

Babylonian Literature
Lectures Delivered at the Royal Institution
By Sayce, A. H.
ISBN 13: 978-1-60608-827-2
Publication date 7/13/2009
Previously published by Samuel Bagster and Sons, 1879

BABYLONIAN LITERATURE.

AMONG the achievements of modern science there is none more remarkable than the decipherment of the cuneiform or wedge-shaped inscriptions of Assyria and Babylonia. A century ago their very existence was unknown, and the few Babylonian seals and bricks that found their way into the hands of travellers were supposed to be inscribed, not with written characters, but with ornamental designs. On the sacred rock of Behistun, where Darius Hystaspis left enduring memorials of himself and his conquered rivals, Sir Robert Ker Porter saw Tiglath-Pileser and the ten tribes, and Keppel the portraiture of Esther and her attendants. The elder Niebuhr published the first exact copies of the cuneiform inscriptions of Persia, but he sacrificed his eyesight to the work. In 1798 Tychsen of Rostock hazarded the conjecture that the characters were alphabetical and to be read from right to left; while Lichtenstein laid down that in their various combinations only one was essential, the rest being added by way of ornament. In the first year of the present century, however, Grotefend, then a young scholar at Bonn, discovered the clue that has since conducted us through the labyrinth of cuneiform decipherment. Following in the steps of Tychsen, he showed that the Persian cuneiform legends were written in an alphabet of forty letters, and that the words were divided from one another by oblique wedges. By comparing several inscriptions together he came to the conclusion that a particular word at the beginning of each, found always in a certain group of monuments, but replaced by another word in another group, must be a royal name; and as the buildings of Persepolis were known to have been erected by the Achæmenian princes, he concluded that the royal name must be that of Cyrus or one of his successors. On assigning conjectural values to the characters in these words, he obtained the names of Darius, Xerxes, Artaxerxes, and Cyrus, and had the satisfaction of finding that the character required by his hypothesis was always in its right place. A certain number of letters was thus ascertained, and the word which invariably followed the royal name could now be read. This eventually turned out to be *khshāyathiya*, answering to the word which in Zend, the old language of Persia, signified "a king." A solid foundation had thus been laid by the genius of Grotefend for the decipherment of the Persian inscriptions; his guess had been confirmed by the results; but it needed another generation before the task was again taken up and carried to completion. Meanwhile the great French scholar Burnouf had founded Zend philology, and an important assistance was thus provided for future students of the Persian cuneiform. Burnouf, himself, published a memoir on the inscriptions of Hamadán; Rask identified two new characters; and finally professor Lassen of Bonn, a colossus of Oriental learning, corrected the results of his predecessors, drew up a fairly complete alphabet of some 39 characters, and translated the inscriptions at that time known in Europe. By the strange coincidence which so often marks a great discovery, at the very moment that Lassen was preparing his memoir at Bonn, a young English officer, now Sir Henry Rawlinson, was independently arriving at the same conclusions in Persia itself. The sculptured tablets of Hamadán, copied by himself, furnished him with the first materials for his researches, and the long inscription of Behistun, with its numerous proper names enabled him to complete the task of decipherment. When the alphabets obtained by Lassen and Rawlinson were compared together, it was found that they differed only in the value assigned to a single letter.

The key had thus been found to the inscriptions of Darius and his successors, and all that remained was to finish what had been so successfully begun. The discovery that the characters might be sounded with inherent vowels achieved the work on the alphabetic side, and a careful comparison of the language thus unexpectedly revealed with Zend and Sanskrit made it as easy to translate the Persian cuneiform inscriptions as a page of the Old Testament.

But new labours awaited the explorer. Side by

side with the Persian legends, ran two others, each in cuneiform characters, which differed considerably, however, from those used by the Persian scribes. The words were not divided from one another as in the Achæmenian texts, while the number of characters employed seemed almost inexhaustible. But nothing is too hard for the human mind, when once in possession of a true method, and little by little the two transcripts which accompanied the Persian version were made to yield up their secrets also. Darius was in the same position as the Turkish Pasha of to-day who publishes an edict for the various races under his charge. The edict has to be drawn up in three separate languages, agglutinative Turkish, Semitic Arabic, and Aryan Persian. And so, too, it was in the old days of the Achæmenian monarchy. The Persian princes wished the inscriptions they had caused to be engraved with so much care to be read by all their subjects, and the Persian text accordingly was always accompanied by translations into the languages of Babylonia and Susiana. The Babylonians spoke the same Semitic language as their northen kinsmen the Assyrians, and this language was Semitic and closely allied to Hebrew, while the Turanian population of Susiana used dialects which resembled those of the modern Finns or Tatars. The proper names, which occurred so frequently in the Persian texts, enabled the inscriptions that stood at their side to be deciphered, and it was then found that the multitude of the characters they contained was due to their being written, not in alphabetic letters, but in characters each of which denoted a syllable. The surprise of the decipherers may be imagined when they discovered that in the one text an agglutinative idiom revealed itself, and in the other a language which seemed almost as familiar as that of the Hebrew Bible. The only difficulty presented by the latter was that the same character appeared to be employed for more than one sound.

The conjecture that this language was the tongue of Babylonia and Assyria was confirmed in an unexpected way. The site of ancient Nineveh was excavated, first by the Frenchman Botta, and then by the Englishman Layard, and a buried city with its palaces, its sculptures and its monuments of ancient life and industry was brought to light. More precious however than even the bas-reliefs that lined the walls of the palaces were the inscriptions that ran across them, for these turned out to be written in the same kind of cuneiform characters and in the same language as the Semitic transcripts of the Persian texts. Time and patience, therefore, were all that were needed to unravel their mysteries and make them disclose their meaning. A few cuneiform inscriptions from Babylonia were already in England, and though most of the characters employed in them differed slightly from those of Nineveh or Behistun, a comparison of texts soon enabled the decipherer to overcome all difficulties, and Dr. Hincks found himself able to read the name of Nebuchadnezzar and the record of his buildings.

But hardly had the first bas-reliefs from Nineveh excited the wonder of the English public, or the clue been found to the inscriptions of Nebuchadnezzar, when two very startling discoveries were made. The first was the existence of a library in ancient Nineveh, a library contained, indeed, not in books but on tablets of burnt clay; yet, nevertheless, a veritable library with works on all the various branches of learning and science that were known to the Assyrians. The other was the revelation of an ancient language, the very existence of which had been previously unsuspected, but which turns out to have been the language of the primitive Chaldeans, the builders of the great cities of Babylonia, the inventors of the cuneiform system of writing, and the originators of the art and civilisation of which the Assyrians were but the heirs and imitators. The language was agglutinative like that of the modern Finns or Turks, an earlier form, in fact, of the class of tongues to which the Susianian inscriptions belong, and it seems to have become extinct before the 17th century B.C. The monarchs who reigned during the preceding epoch call themselves kings of "Sumir and Accad," or of "the land of Accad," and since Sumir, the Shinar of the Bible, was the first part of the country occupied by the invading Semites, while Accad long continued to be regarded as the seat of an alien race, the language and population of primitive Chaldea have been named Accadian by the majority of Assyrian scholars. The part played by these Accadians in the intellectual history of mankind is highly important. They were the earliest civilisers of Western Asia, and it is to them that we have to trace the arts and sciences, the religious traditions, and the philosophy not only of the Assyrians, but also of the Phœnicians, the Aramæans, and even the Hebrews themselves. It was, too, from Chaldea that the germs of Greek art and of much of the Greek pantheon and mythology originally came. Columnar architecture reached its first and highest development in Babylonia; the lions that still guard the main entrance of Mykenæ are distinctly Assyrian in character; and the Greek Herakles with his twelve labours finds his prototype in the hero of the great Chaldean epic. It is difficult to say how much of our present culture is not owed to the stunted, oblique-eyed people of ancient Babylonia; Jerusalem and Athens are the sacred cities of our modern life; and both Jerusalem and Athens were profoundly influenced by the ideas which had their first starting-point in primæval Accad. The Semite has ever been a trader and an intermediary, and his earliest work was the precious trade in spiritual and mental wares. Babylonia was the home and mother of Semitic culture and Semitic inspiration; the Phœnicians never forgot that they were a colony from the Persian Gulf, while the Israelite recounted that his father Abraham had been born in Ur of the Chaldees.

Almost the whole of the Assyrian literature was derived from Accad, and translated from the dead language of primitive Chaldea. The Assyrians have been aptly termed the Romans of ancient Asia; they were a nation of soldiers and legislators, not of thinkers and scribes. Like the characters in which they wrote, their art and science and literature were borrowed from Babylonia. When at length they turned their attention to the arts of peace, and began to cultivate a "learned leisure," they were content to imitate slavishly their Babylonian model, to establish libraries like those of Chaldea, and to furnish them with the plunder of the ancient libraries of Erech, Sippara, and other cities. Their very temples were built of brick in imitation of those of Babylonia, though stone was plentiful in Assyria; and the clay literature of Nineveh perpetuated the clay literature of the alluvial plains of the south.

It is impossible to say when and where the first library of Accad was founded. Berosus makes Pantibibla, the town of books, the chief antediluvian city of Babylonia, and the home of Amelon, the third fabulous monarch of Chaldea. Sisuthrus, the Chaldean Noah, too, is made to bury his books at Sippara before the Deluge, and disentomb them after the descent from the ark; a legend in which, perhaps, we may trace the influence of a false etymology of Sippara from the Semitic *sepher* "a book." The library of Erech, the modern Warka, was among the oldest in Chaldea, and from it came the epic of Gisdhubar, and the story of the flood, of which several copies were made for the library at Nineveh. Excavation may yet uncover the library of Ur, now represented by the mounds of Mugheir, and the capital of the first Chaldean empire of which we know. Of the library of Cutha all that remains is a legend of the Creation, and of a war of the giants, while that of Larsa or Senkereh has yielded several mathematical tablets, including tables of squares and cubes. But the most famous of all the libraries of Babylonia was that of Agané, a city near Sippara, founded by Sargon I., probably in the 17th century B.C. It was for this library that the great work on astronomy and astrology in seventy-two books was compiled, which Berosus, it would seem, translated into Greek. The very site of Agané is now unknown, but should explorations be ever made in that part of the country, we may still expect to find there the buried library of Sargon.

Sargon himself was a Semite, the first of the Semitic conquerors, perhaps, who patronised literature. The language of Accad had already ceased to be the tongue of the people; here and there a scribe might possibly be found who still knew how to speak it, but otherwise it was a learned dialect like the Latin of the middle ages. The books, therefore, with which the new library was stocked were either translated from Accadian originals, or else based on Accadian texts, and filled with technical words which belonged to the old language. Education, however, must have been widely spread; the catalogue of the astronomical works in the library of Agané enjoins the reader to write down the number of the tablet or book he needs, and the librarian will thereupon give him the tablet required. What stronger proof than this can we have of the development of literature and education, and of the existence of a considerable reading public? Every tablet had its number and its place, and the tablets were arranged according to subject and contents. The arrangement adopted by Sargon's librarians, one of whom has left us a signet-ring, now in the British Museum,[1] must have been the product of generations of former experience. They simply inherited the labours and wisdom of their Accadian predecessors, just as their monarch himself inherited the organised rule and royal prerogatives of the Accadian princes. With affected archaism they gave him the Accadian title of *dadhrum* "the deviser," and styled him further in their own language "the king of justice, the deviser of justice, and the deviser of prosperity."[2] Yet Sargon, whose very name signified "the established king," seems to have been an usurper and sprung from the people. A curious legend of his infancy has been preserved, which assimilates him to Perseus and Romulus, to Moses and other popular heroes of antiquity. "My mother," it makes him say, "was an outcast, my father I knew not, my father's brother ruled the land. In the city Azupirānu, on the bank of the river Euphrates, my mother the outcast conceived me; in a hiding-place she bore me. She laid me in an ark of rushes, with bitumen (its) mouth she closed. She gave me to the river, which drowned me not. The river carried me; to Acci the ferryman did it bring me. Acci the ferryman in the tenderness of his heart, lifted me up. Acci the ferryman as his own child nurtured me. Acci the ferryman as his woodsman made me. And in my woodsmanship did the goddess Istar love me."[3]

In spite of this later myth, however, which has fastened upon his name, Sargon was a historical

[1] Nitakh-Anu or Lugur-Ana, son of Gantu. (*W. A. I.* I., 3, 11.)

[2] *W. A. I.* II., 48, 40.

[3] *W. A. I.* III., 4, 7.

king, who has left us contemporaneous monuments. His conquests were carried far and wide. He defeated the Elamites and the Hittites of Northern Syria, he set up a record of his deeds on the shores of the Mediterranean, he reduced the independent states of Babylonia under his sway, and after suppressing a formidable revolt that had broken out at home claimed to be the sovereign of the four regions of the world. His son, Naram-Sin, continued the career of his father, and acquired the turquoise mines of Maganna, the peninsula of Sinai. His subjects, in the extravagance of their adulation, raised him to the rank of deity, like the emperors of Rome in later days; and a cylinder of black hæmatite, found by General di Cesnola among the treasures of the Cyprian Kurium, has survived to tell us of the fact. But the glory of Sargon's dynasty was short-lived. His second successor was a queen, whose throne was overturned by Khammuragas, the chief of a Kossæan horde of invaders from Elam. Khammuragas established his rule over the whole of Babylonia, and Babylon for the first time became a capital city, a position which it retained for more than a thousand years. It was about this time, probably, that the Babylonian library was founded, from which came the original of a Babylonian fragment on astronomy, written partly on papyrus, partly on clay. The papyrus has long since perished both there and elsewhere, and the clay tablets alone have resisted the assaults of time. Most of the contents of this library appear to have been carried off to Assyria when Babylon was taken and destroyed by

Sennacherib B.C. 695; the rest would have perished in the ruins of the city, which burnt for three days, the Araxes, the river of Babylon, being afterwards filled with the débris that survived the conflagration. The libraries that may yet lie buried beneath the site belong to the Babylon of Nebuchadnezzar, and probably owe their foundation to him.

Throughout the larger part of the period occupied by the second Assyrian Empire, that is to say, from the reign of Tiglath-Pileser II. to the fall of Nineveh, the intellectual activity of Babylonia was transferred to Assyria. Distracted by civil war, and harassed by foreign invaders, the country could no longer support its libraries and the observatories and universities which accompanied them. Time after time was Babylonia overrun by Caldai or Chaldeans from the Persian Gulf, by the Semitic nomads from Arabia, by the Assyrians from the north, and by Elamites from the east; it became the battle-ground of the great nations of Asia; and when the Assyrians at last obtained peaceable possession of it, they found a land wasted with fire and sword, its cities ruined, and its population half-extinct. Meanwhile the libraries of Assyria had been prospering at the expense of those of Babylonia. The primitive capital of the country, Assur, now Kalah-Sherghat, built in the Accadian epoch as its name, which means "water-bank," declares, no doubt possessed a library which still awaits the spade of the excavator. But the first Assyrian library of which we know was that of Calah, a city built by Shalmaneser I. about B.C. 1300 and restored by Assur-natsir-pal in 885. It was after its second foundation that the library was established there, and among other books deposited in it was a copy of the great work on astronomy. The collection was presided over by Nabu-zukup-cinu, the son of Merodach-mubasa, "the astronomer," from the 6th year of Sargon (B.C. 716), to the 22nd year of Sennacherib (B. 684), and the work of copying and composing texts went on briskly.

It remained for Assur-bani-pal or Sardanapalus, the son of Essar-haddon, the "Grand Monarque" of Assyria and the great patron of literature, to surpass his predecessors, and gather into his library at Nineveh or Kouyunjik the selected literary treasures of Babylonia and Assyria. Scribes were kept busily engaged in copying and translating earlier works, or in drawing up new ones either in Assyrian or in the extinct Accadian, the study of which was now revived. In fact, grammars, dictionaries, and phrase-books, of the old language were compiled, the Assyrian equivalents being written interlineally or in the right-hand column. To facilitate the study of the literature, as well as to assist the strangers from Egypt or Cyprus or Lydia who thronged the court of Sardanapalus, syllabaries were made, in which the cuneiform characters were classified and arranged. The despatches of governors and generals, the correspondence of the royal family, the petitions which were presented to the king, were all carefully copied out and deposited on special shelves of the library. The decaying literature of Babylonia was forwarded to Nineveh, and the Assyrian scribes were entrusted with the task of copying and re-editing it. A new text was the most valuable present a

Babylonian city could send, and it was prized with almost the same enthusiasm as a classical MS. in the age of the Renaissance. With reiterated earnestness the king declares that Nebo "the prophet" god of literature, and his wife Tasmit, "the hearer," had made broad his ears and given sight to his eyes so that he had "regard to the engraved characters of the tablets;" and the writing, which none of the kings before him had cared for, even "the secrets of Nebo, the literature of the library as much as was suitable, "on tablets" he had "written, engraved and explained, and stored in the midst of his palace for the inspection of" his "subjects."

The last words show plainly the extent to which education had been carried, and suggest that the librarians of Assur-bani-pal were not allowed much leisure. They could have had little difficulty, however, in finding the books that were wanted; the library was organised very completely, and the fragments of the catalogue that we possess show that the tablets were arranged methodically: nine of the hymns to the gods, for instance, being placed on the west side, and fifteen others on the east side. Every tablet was numbered and marked, and where there was a series of them dealing with the same subject, each concluded with the first line of the whole series and sometimes also with the first line of the next tablet. Thus the Deluge tablet finishes with the words "the 11th tablet of the series beginning 'the hero Gisdhubar had seen the fountain,'" and prefixes to this the first line of the twelfth tablet: "the gadfly in the house of the serving-man he left."

It is this library of Assur-bani-pal's which has yielded most of what we know about the literature and the history of Babylonia and Assyria. The present mounds of Kouyunjik mark the site of the palace of which it formed part, and the broken débris of tablets which have fallen from the upper floor where they were originally kept are the most precious relics that have come down to us of the Assyrian Empire. They were first discovered by Mr. Layard in 1850, and several chests filled with the fragments were sent to England. Their nature and importance were at once recognised by Sir. H. Rawlinson, but it was not until after Mr. George Smith's appointment at the British Museum that the last chest was unpacked, the last broken pieces examined and ticketed, and the laborious work of piecing them together made fairly complete. The discovery of a number of fragments belonging to different editions of the Chaldean story of the Deluge revived the public interest in Assyrian matters, and Mr. Smith was despatched, first by the proprietors of the *Daily Telegraph*, and then by the Trustees of the British Museum, to re-open the trenches at Kouyunjik and unearth the remainder of Assur-bani-pal's library. This was the ultimate object of the ill-fated expedition of last year; and it is to be hoped that notwithstanding Mr. Smith's death the object may yet be achieved. Many of the fragments in the British Museum are now useless because the portions needed to complete them are still lying buried under their native soil; others of them tell us but half their tale, and break off frequently just where it is of most interest and importance to know the sequel. When the whole of the great library of Nineveh has been excavated and collected anew in the British Museum, we may then explore those far older libraries of Babylonia with their stores of literature of which the contents of Assur-bani-pal's were but the selected residuum.

It is, however, to the library of Assur-bani-pal that we have at present to look for the best part of our knowledge of Babylonian literature. Its character was various in the extreme. Historical and mythological documents, religious records, legal, geographical, astronomical, and astrological treatises; poetical compositions, grammatical and lexical disquisitions, lists of stones and trees, of birds and beasts, copies of treaties, of commercial transactions, of correspondence, of petitions to the king, and of royal proclamations, such were the chief contents of this strange old library. The larger portion of the religious and poetical works were translations from Accadian, the original text being generally given side by side with the Assyrian rendering. Let us first turn our attention to the historical literature, a good deal of which is, contrary to the usual rule, of purely Assyrian origin.

History is little more than a collection of disconnected facts or of isolated biographies without chronology, the skeleton upon which it must be built. We cannot trace the connection between events or determine their development unless we know the relative dates to which they must be assigned. A system of chronology is as indispensable to the historian as the framework is to the scene that is painted thereon. Now the library of Kouyunjik is fortunately rich in chronological tablets. Assyrian history rests upon a solid foundation, and we are not left to reconstruct it with the doubtful aid of genealogies, and the still more doubtful aid of conjecture. In this respect the Assyrian scholar is more fortunate than the Egyptologist. Some fourteen years ago Sir H. Rawlinson found, among the broken tablets at the Museum, the remains of several copies of an Assyrian Canon, which fixes both the succession and the dates of the later kings of Assyria. The years were marked by the names of certain officers, who corresponded with the eponymous archons of Athens, and after whom the years were named. In the earlier period of the Canon the king himself was eponyme in his first year, and throughout the document the end of a reign is noted by a broad horizontal line. The fragments of the Canon that we possess do not carry us beyond the year 909 B.C., but a regular chronology had been kept for centuries previously, as may be seen from the fact that inscriptions of Rimmon-nirari I. (B.C. 1320), and Tiglath-Pileser I. (B.C. 1120), are each dated by the name of an eponyme. Besides this Canon which simply records the lapse of time, there is another in which the chief events of each year are added to the name, or rather the title, of its eponyme. We learn from this second Canon that the privilege of naming the year passed in a kind of rotation among the officers of the Assyrian court. It is questionable whether this mode of reckoning time by eponymes was not due to the practical genius of the Assyrians themselves; at all events, we have not yet come across any traces of such a system in Babylonia. The Babylonians, however, had a chronology of their own; they dated from particular eras; and the British Museum possesses part of a list of Chaldean monarchs and dynasties, in which the years and months of each king's reign, as well as of the several dynasties, are given with great exactness. Perhaps an Assyrian scribe would have counted among the chronological works of the library a curious document of Assyrian origin, in which the various wars and treaties between the Assyrians and the Babylonians are briefly recorded. As the narrative is always to the credit of the Assyrians, the document can hardly have been palateable to a Babylonian reader.

The history of Assyria, so far as the conquests and triumphs of its rulers are concerned, may be read on the bas-reliefs that lined the walls of their palaces, or in the clay-cylinders which they buried under the foundation-stones of their buildings. But the royal library contained much besides, which is more valuable to the modern historian than all these annals of war and victory. Here were deposited the letters that passed between allied or hostile sovereigns; here were stored the petitions of private individuals, the despatches of generals in the field, the texts of treaties, and the omens which the augurs declared to be favourable to the undertakings of the king. Here, too, was preserved the private will of Sennacherib, before his favourite son Essar-haddon had become heir presumptive, in which he leaves him in the safe keeping of the temple of Nebo bracelets, coronets and other objects of gold, ivory, and precious stones, as well as the curious lesson in spelling received by one of the grand-daughters of Assur-banipal, who is told not to write *umpici*, or to say *impuci*. The petitions received by the king were numerous. One of them illustrates the despotic power of the monarch, and the slavish submission of his subjects. A political prisoner, Nebo-balatsu-ikbi by name, after invoking various gods to prosper Sardanapalus, goes on to ask, "why once and even twice do I present my prayer to the king, though no one has told me to do so?" and then complains that though the people of Babylonia had committed sin "against the king my lord, I committed no sin against the king my lord," but, on the contrary, "went and declared the command of the king unto Arrabi (the rebel), saying: (This) news is agreeable to the palace (Porte)." The prisoner, it seems, had to make several journeys between the Assyrian court and the enemy, the result of which was, that although he had "seized the feet of the king, and bowed his face unto death," the monarch was made to believe in his complicity with the insurgents, and accordingly adjudged him to death. By a judicious use of his gold, however, he obtained a respite of two days, and meanwhile the Assyrian king so far relented as to substitute imprisonment for immediate execution. Even this, however, was not to the liking of a man who persisted in protesting his innocence.[1]

Some interesting fragments, found by Mr. Smith

[1] *W. A. I.* IV., 5, 3, 2.

shortly before starting on his last journey, appear to relate to the closing period of the Assyrian Empire. They are merely the first rough copies of the king's proclamation, which were never re-written, and are consequently somewhat hard to read. A great coalition from the north was menacing the monarchy. Kaztaritu of Carukassu, in whom perhaps we may see Kyaxares of Media, with the Gimirrai or Cimmerians, and the tribes of Minni or Van, and of Saparda, on the coast of the Euxine, had attacked Assyria, defeated her armies, and taken by storm her frontier cities. Nineveh itself was threatened, and its king Essar-haddon, the Saracus of the Greek writers, had proclaimed a solemn fast to the gods in the extremity of his despair. But the gods had deserted the cause of Assyria, and before long the desolater had herself become desolate, and her last sovereign had perished, if we may trust classical tradition, on the funeral pyre of his own palace.

The second Assyrian Empire had not lasted a century and a half. It owed its origin to Tiglath-Pileser II., who seized the throne in B.C. 747 and inaugurated that system of Satrapies which was afterwards perfected by the Persian Darius. Founded by an usurper it was perpetuated by usurpation and murder. Its three first rulers, Tiglath-Pileser, Shalmaneser and Sargon, were all successful generals, unrelated one to the other. Tiglath-Pileser as well as Shalmaneser were probably assassinated; we know from the inscriptions that such was the fate of both Sargon and Sennacherib. Essar-haddon after having to secure his throne by a war with his two elder brothers ended by abdicating; while it was under his successor Assur-bani-pal that the great revolt broke out which shook Assyria to its foundations and ushered in the decline of an Empire which had extended from the borders of India to Lydia and Nubia, had penetrated into the heart of Arabia and the snows of the Caucasus, and had made the ancient kingdoms of Babylonia and Egypt tributary provinces.

The first Empire had been handed down in orderly succession from father to son, and been established by the conquests of Assur-natsir-pal and Shalmaneser II. in the 9th century B.C. But it was an Empire of merely military occupation. The states overrun by the Assyrian arms rose into rebellion as soon as the standards of the victorious army were out of sight. No attempt was made to organise and amalgamate the countries that had been subdued. Their government was left unchanged, and the Assyrian general contented himself with sacking their cities and carrying off their treasures to Nineveh. Though the Assyrian armies marched in triumph through Mesopotamia and Armenia, through Babylonia and Palestine, the only result of this waste of life and energy was the introduction of the cuneiform system of writing into Armenia and western Mesopotamia. There was as yet no social contact and cohesion between the Assyrians and their conquered neighbours, and as soon as disorder broke out in Assyria, or the monarch ceased to be a man of action, the Empire found itself contracted to the neighbourhood of Nineveh itself.

Assur-natsir-pal, however, was not the first of the Assyrian conquerors. He had had a predecessor in Tiglath-Pileser I., whose date is fixed by later inscriptions at B.C. 1130. Tiglath-Pileser had spent his life in fighting, in hunting and in building, and so had left a model for all future Assyrian kings to follow. He had hunted wild bulls in the neighbourhood of Carchemish, the great Hittite capital, had reduced Comagene and penetrated into Cilicia, had swept Asia Minor as far as the Halys, defeating on his way the Moschi and Tibareni, the Meshech and Tubal of Scripture, whose territories extended much further to the south than in the later days of classical geography, and had contended with Babylonia and the nations of the east. But Tiglath-Pileser was something more than a conqueror, and we learn from his records that he established botanical gardens in Assyria and endeavoured to acclimatise the vegetable products of the countries he had overrun. Thus he tells us that as for "the cedar, the *liccarin* tree and the almug, from the countries I have conquered, these trees which none of the kings, my fathers, that were before me, had planted, I took, and in the plantations of my land I planted, and by the name of plantation I called them; whatsoever in my land there was not I took (and) the plantations of Assyria I established."[1]

A predecessor of Tiglath-Pileser, Tiglath-Adar, had captured Babylon about 1270 B.C., and founded there the dynasty which Berosus, the Chaldean historian, called Assyrian. For a time Assyria and Babylonia

[1] *W. A. I.* I., 15, 16-27.

were under the sway of one sceptre, but only for a time. The Babylonians never forgot that they were the older kingdom of which Assyria had once been an outlying province, and they were, therefore, specially impatient of the Assyrian yoke. Assyria, in fact, had first become an independent monarchy in the 17th century B.C., when Chaldea was conquered by Khammuragas and his Kossæans, and the dynasty founded which Tiglath-Adar had overthrown. Assyria took its name from its primitive capital Assur; and Babylonian monuments still exist which go back to a period when the future Assyria was but a part of the vast half-barbarous region of Gutium, the Goyim of Genesis, of which Tidal or Turgal was king. It was in the eastern part of Gutium that the land of Nizir was situated, on the highest peak of which, the present Mount Elwand, the ark of the Chaldean Noah was believed to have rested.

The beginning of Chaldean history is lost in a fabulous antiquity. The earliest princes whose inscriptions have come down to us are those of Ur on the western bank of the Euphrates. Here was the seat of the first monarchs of all Chaldea who assumed the imperial title of "kings of Sumir and Accad." It was under Lig-Bagas (?) and his son Dungi, that the petty states of Babylonia were suppressed, and great buildings erected like the Temple of the Moon-god at Ur. But the Semite was already in the land. Sumir or Shinar, with its four cities, had passed from the possession of the Accadians into the hands of Semitic conquerors. Even in Accad itself the power of the old race was on the decline, and the fall of the supremacy of Ur brought with it the final overthrow of Accadian rule. The Accadai or "Highlanders," for such is the meaning of their name, must have descended from the mountains of Elam at a very early epoch, and imposed their domination upon their more peaceable kinsfolk, the Sumerians. The country was divided between the newcomers in the south, and the old population in the north, and at a later period, when the northern Sumer came to be occupied by Semites, the geographical distinction between Sumer and Accad became also a linguistic one. It is probable that it was the Accadians rather than the Sumerians to whom was due the invention of the picture writing, out of which the cuneiform characters were to spring. At any rate the same ideograph that signified country in general also signified "mountain," and the want of a special character to denote the palm-tree would imply that the framers of the writing were not yet acquainted with the sunny plains of Babylonia and their principal product. The legends, too, which brought the earliest civilisers of the country, the instructors of Chaldea in art and science and writing, from the waters of the Persian Gulf, point in the same direction.

Babylonian history had a large background of myth. Ten kings were enumerated before the flood whose reigns occupied 432,000 years, while the ages that succeeded that event were peopled by heroes whose exploits formed the subject of a whole cycle of romance. It was in the antediluvian period that the strange composite creatures, half men, half fish, were made to ascend from the ocean and teach the tribes of Babylonia the rudiments of civilised life. The tablets in the library of Kouyunjik contain one reference only, so far as we know, to these mythical teachers of Chaldea. A quotation from an Accadian text, embodied in the Assyrian reading-book of the old language,[1] states how "their god to the waters they restored, to the house of (his) gifts he descended." The librarians of Nineveh, it would seem, cared but little for these antiquities of the southern kingdom. They preferred the more stirring adventures of the great solar hero whom we will provisionally call Gisdhubar, or of the giant kings Etanna and Ner whose phantoms still held rule in Hades. Babylonia before the Deluge possessed scanty interest for them in comparison with Babylonia after the Deluge, when Assyria, with its 350 monarchs, whom Sargon enumerates as his predecessors, could partake in some measure of its mythical glories.

Sisuthrus, Etanna, Tammuz, and Gisdhubar were the four heroes whose deeds the poets and scribes of the historic period loved to commemorate. Gisdhubar especially, whom Mr. Smith has shown good reason for identifying with Nimrod, was the subject of numberless legends and lays. It is his adventures which form the connecting thread in that great Babylonian epic which incorporates the story of the flood and the ark wherein Sisuthrus was saved. The epic is in twelve books, arranged upon an astronomical principle, each book answering to an appropriate sign of the zodiac and month of the Accadian year.

[1] *W. A. I.* II., 16, 58, 59.

Thus the story of the Deluge is an episode of the eleventh book, which corresponds with the sign Aquarius and "the rainy month" of the Accadian calendar, while the sixth lay which relates the love and wrath of the goddess Istar harmonises with Virgo, the sixth sign of the zodiac and "the month of the errand of Istar," the sixth month of the year. This agreement between the subject-matter of the several lays or books and the names of the zodiacal signs and months in the Accadian, though not in the Assyrian, calendar, shows pretty plainly that the epic was a composition of the Accadian period; and the conclusion is confirmed by the colophon added to each book of the poem by the Assyrian scribe. We may safely infer that the present text is a Semitic translation of an Accadian original, even though the original itself is no longer extant. As Accadian had become a dead language before the era of Sargon of Agane and the 17th century B.C., we are carried back into a hoar antiquity for this Homer of Chaldea. But the epic in twelve books was itself the work of a later stage of Accadian literature. It is an artificial product, a redaction of previously existing lays relating to Gisdhubar and his companions. The very legend of the Deluge, which is embodied in the poem, is an amalgamation of at least two different versions of the tale; sometimes the same words are repeated with only a change from the first to the third person; sometimes contradictions occur as when the flood of waters is ascribed, now to the Sun-god, now to Hea, and now again to Bel; sometimes the same statement is expressed twice over in slightly varying language,—all showing the unskilful work of a redactor. The independent lays incorporated in the epic of Gisdhubar were not, however, the sole poems relating to the Deluge which were current in primæval Babylonia, and fragments of others have been discovered among the débris of Assur-bani-pal's library. But what a long interval of time is implied by the composition of these old poems, the combination of two or three of them into a whole, and the subsequent inclusion of that whole among the adventures of Gisdhubar! Like all national epics, the epic of ancient Chaldea was a slow growth, and in its final form was pieced together out of earlier materials. For the first origin of the lays, which told of Sisuthrus or of Gisdhubar, we must go back to a past that was already half-forgotten in the days of Abraham and the monarchs of Ur.

Now Gisdhubar is plainly a solar hero. His twelve adventures, like the twelve labours of Herakles, mark the passage of the sun through the twelve months of the year. And as the sickening sun of winter, so, too, Gisdhubar sickens in the autumnal month of October, and not until he has bathed in the waters of the eastern ocean does he once more recover strength and brilliance with the beginning of the new year. The books of the epic take us through all the zodiacal signs: the lion that Gisdhubar slays is the zodiacal Leo; his seer Hea-bani, half-man, half-bull, is brought to him in the second month of the Accadian year, that of "the propitious bull," presided over by Taurus; he is wooed by Istar under the sign of Virgo; the encircling ocean is reached in the tenth month of "the setting sun;" and his lamentation over the corpse of Hea-bani is made in "the dark month" of Adar, the last of the year, when the twin "fish of Hea" accompany the sun.[1] But Gisdhubar is but the prototype and model of the Greek Herakles. Like the germs of Greek art, the germs of much of the Greek pantheon and of Greek mythology have been traced back to Babylonia, along the high-road of culture and civilisation that ran across Asia Minor, or through the fostering hands of Phœnicia and its colonies. Herakles is the Melkarth, the Sun-god, of Tyre, whose temple had been founded there 2300 years before Herodotus visited the merchant-city. And the story of Herakles was but a repetition of the older story of Gisdhubar. Hea-bani, the confidant and adviser of the Chaldean hero, is the centaur Kheiron, the instructor of Herakles; for Kheiron was the son of Kronos, and Kronos, we are told, was the Babylonian Hea, the "creator" of Hea-bani. The lion that Gisdhubar slew is the lion of Nemea; the winged bull that Anu made to avenge the slight of his daughter Istar is the bull of Krete; the tyrant Khumbaba slain by Gisdhubar in "the land of the pine-trees, the seat of the gods, the sanctuary of the spirits," is the tyrant Geryon; the gems borne by the trees of the forest, beyond "the gateway of the sun," are the apples of the Hesperides; and the deadly sickness of Gisdhubar himself is but the fever caused by the poisonous tunic of Nessus. Long before the Greek poets began to weave the gorgeous web of their

[1] *W. A. I.* III., 53, 2, 13.

wondrous mythology, the poets of Accad had been busy at the same work, and the woof that lay before them had been the same. There in ancient Accad had been all the materials out of which the richest poetry and the wildest romance might be devised, and the fragments we possess of the Gisdhubar epic are a marvellous storchouse of myth and legend. Here we may learn how Gisdhubar dreamed that the stars fell from heaven and struck him on the back, while a lion-like monster stood over him; how Zaidu the hunter failed to bring Hea-bani from his savage hermitage, and how the seer, like another Merlin, was finally enticed to Erech by the two handmaids of Istar, whose names signify "the devotee" and "the smiling one;" how Istar was taunted with her many bridegrooms, Tammuz the young and beautiful sun-god, Alala the wild eagle, the lion-son of Silele, and Isullanu the woodsman; how Gisdhubar wandered to the boundaries of the world, where scorpion-men guard the gate of the sun, "their crown at the lattice of heaven, under hell their feet," and then on through the sandy desert, "the pathway of the sun," and the forest where the trees, like that of Vergil with the golden bough, bore precious gems as fruit, until he reached the borders of the sea and the ocean-gates, over which the women Sabitu and Siduri "the eye of youth" keep eternal watch; how he met the Chaldean Charon, with whom he sailed to Datilla, the river of death, where he beheld Sisuthrus, the hero of the Deluge, in the abode of the blessed; and how, finally, Hea-bani was slain by the poisonous gad-fly, and lay in the dark and dismal region of Hades until Merodach, the sun-god, came at the prayer of Gisdhubar, and the ghost of Hea-bani mounted up from the earth and passed to the heaven of heroes, where, like the Norse Vikings in their Valhalla, they feast on couches and drink the pure waters of life. It was here, in "the land of the silver sky," as they called it, that the court poets of Nineveh prayed that their monarch might find his eternal home.

Sisuthrus, the hero of the Deluge, was no less famous in Babylonian legend than Gisdhubar himself. His Accadian name means "the sun of life," "the morning sun," and his father's name Ubara-tutu, "the glow of sunset," unmistakeably proclaims his solar character. His birthplace was Suripkhu or Surippak, the Larankha of the Greek copyists, a famous city of primæval Accad. It was here that Hea, the god of the deep, warned Sisuthrus of the flood of waters with which the wickedness of mankind was about to be punished, and bade him build a ship 600 cubits long, and 60 cubits broad and high. The pious Sisuthrus obeyed the divine command, and after pitching the vessel within and without, and offering up a sacrifice to the gods, he entered the ship with his people and his servants, his treasure and the beasts of the field. For seven days the storm lasted, while the pilot Buzur-sadi-rabi, "the strength (?) of the mighty mountain," steered the ark; the earth was covered with an overwhelming deluge, and the storm-clouds traversed mountain and plain, carrying ruin and destruction in their path. All life was destroyed from off the face of the earth, and the gods themselves fled in terror to the highest "heaven of Anu." At last, however, the flood was ended, and Sisuthrus opened the window of his ark, and the light broke over his face. But there was a waste desolation on all sides; nothing might be seen save the troubled waters and the corpses which floated on their surface. The ark finally rested on the mountain of Nizir, "the mountain of the world," the present Elwend, where the Accadians placed the cradle of their race, and believed that, like another Olympus, it was the habitation of the gods, and the pivot of heaven. Then the Chaldean Noah sent forth first a dove and after that a swallow, but, as in the Biblical narrative, they could find no resting-place for their feet, and returned to the ship. Next a raven was despatched from the ark, and it found food in the floating corpses, "it wandered away and did not return." So Sisuthrus knew that the land was dry; and he left the ark, sending forth the animals "to the four winds," and building an altar on the mountain-peak. Here he poured forth bowls of wine by sevens, and the gods "gathered like flies over the sacrifice," descending to the earth by the golden bridge of the rainbow. Then Bel made a covenant with Sisuthrus, and swore not to destroy mankind by the waters of a flood any more. After this Sisuthrus was translated even as the Biblical Enoch had been, along with his wife and people, while the rest of his followers travelled westward, and settled again in the plains of Babylonia.

Here there broke out the great war of which Greek

writers tell us, waged by Titan, Bel, Prometheus, and Ogygus, against Kronos or Hea. Titan may be the Etanna of the inscriptions, whom Istar saw in Hades, where "dwell the chiefs and unconquered ones, the bards and great men, and the monsters of the deep." Etanna, like Sisuthrus, had ruled over Surippak, and seven spirits had been subject to him, like the genii whom eastern fable believes to have worked for Solomon. With the help of these seven spirits he had built a city of brick, which may have been the city where stood the tower whose head was made to reach to heaven. The tower of Babel or Babylon, however, had been the special work of Sar-tuli-elli, "the king of the holy mound," and its erection was placed in the month Tisri at the autumnal equinox. But the heart of the master-builder had been "wicked against the father of all the gods," and the tower had been raised with the unholy purpose of storming the skies. What had been constructed with so much labour during the day, therefore, was blown down by the winds at night; the builders were "confounded" and "scattered abroad," and their counsel and speech were "made strange." For long ages the ruined tower remained a monument of divine vengeance, until at last Nebuchadrezzar, in the height of his glory, determined to finish it, and under the name of the "Temple of the Seven Lights of the Earth," it became the wonder of Borsippa, the suburb of Babylon. Its remains, known as the Birs-i-Nimrud, have long excited the admiration of travellers, and served as a quarry for the inhabitants of the country. When the Semites played upon the name of the neighbouring city, and connected the name of Bab-el, "the gate of the god," with the verb *balbel*, "to confound," the old Accadian name of the place, Ca-dimirra, of which Bab-el was but the Semitic translation, must have been long forgotten.

Manifold were the tales told in Accad of the Titanic races of the ancient world. One of the tablets brought to Nineveh from the library of Cuthah describes how the first creation was one of monsters and giants, "men with the bodies of birds of the desert, human beings with the faces of ravens;" the terrible brood of Tihamat the principle of chaos and night. Among them were seven kings, all brothers, the sons of king Banini and queen Milili, who ruled over a Titanic people 6000 in number. The eldest of the brothers was called "The Thunderbolt," a name which gives us the clue to the atmospheric origin of the legend. With this race of giants, like those of whom we read in the earlier chapters of Genesis, the bright powers of light and day had to wage war; and though the inscription which records the legend is both mutilated and obscure, enough can be made out to show that the seven brothers were at last defeated and destroyed. But the struggle had been a terrible one, and for three successive years army after army had been sent out, never to return.

This war between the giants and the gods, between the representatives of the old anarchic forces of nature, and the new powers of sunlight and order, is but a variant form of the war of the gods, when

Merodach, the sun-god, went forth, armed with a helmet of light and his scimitar, the lightning-flash, to contend with Tihamat, "the deep," and her allies the seven storm-demons. The Chaldean Michael was accompanied by his four divine dogs, and his demon-enemy, who is sometimes called "The Dragon of the Sea," sometimes "The Seven-Headed Serpent," or "The Serpent of Night," proved no match for her mighty antagonist. The sickle-shaped scimitar of Merodach is the ἅρπη of the Greek Perseus, and while on the one hand it is identified with "the star of the bow," it is addressed on the other hand as "the thunderbolt," "the fire-god," "the lightning of battle," "the weapon of fifty heads." On gems and bas-reliefs it is not unfrequently represented as a seven-forked thunderbolt, and like the *shamir*, or worm, no bigger than a barley-corn, which could split the hardest rocks, and by whose aid Solomon built the temple, it is called "The Hero that striketh the Mountains," "that from whose hand the mountain escapes not."[1] It was by means of this wonderful weapon that Tihamat was quelled and immured with all her demoniac forces in the darkness of the underworld.

There was yet another war in heaven, which had been the subject of Accadian poetry from time immemorial. The Chaldeans were a nation of star-gazers, and though, as elsewhere, many of their myths were of solar origin, there were yet many more which disguised but slightly their lunar character. One of those which has come down to us, is a curious

[1] *W. A. I.* II., 19.

legend of the war of the seven evil spirits or storm-clouds against the moon, and the poet who composed it lets us see plainly, from time to time, that its primary reference was to an eclipse. "It was in the revolving days," he says, from the 25th of February to the 3rd of March, "when those wicked gods, the rebel spirits, who in the lower part of heaven had been created, with wicked head devising, extended their rule unto the dawn." They are likened to all the fantastic shapes that the clouds seem to assume, and "the raging wind," it is declared, "has been fiercely bound to them." The attack began "with evil tempest, baleful wind," and "from the foundations of the heavens like the lightning they (darted)." The lower region of the sky was reduced to its primæval chaos, and the gods above sat in anxious council. The moon-god, the sun-god, and the goddess Istar, at once lunar and stellar, had been appointed to sway in close harmony the lower sky, and to command "the hosts of heaven;" but when the moon-god was attacked by the seven spirits of evil, his companions basely forsook him, the sun-god retreating to his place and Istar taking refuge in the highest heaven. But "Bel beheld the eclipse of the hero, the moon-god, in heaven," and sent his messenger Nebo in haste to ask advice of Hea, the god of wisdom. And "Hea called his son, Merodach, and the word he spake: 'Go, my son Merodach! The light of sky, my son, even the moon-god, is grievously darkened in heaven, and in eclipse from heaven is vanishing. Those seven wicked gods, the serpents of death, who fear not," are waging unequal war with the labouring moon. Merodach obeyed his father's bidding, and in "glistering armour of unsoiled cloths and broad raiment," with his "helmet of light like the fire" upon his head, successfully overthrew the seven powers of darkness.

Such is an outline of the poem in which this curious legend is recorded, and we are fortunate in possessing the Accadian text of it as well as the later Assyrian translation. This, however, is not the only poem in which the deeds of the seven evil spirits are recorded. A long hymn to the god of fire, composed by an Accadian poet of Eridhu, recounts how "those seven in the mountain of the sunset were begotten: those seven in the mountain of the sunrise did grow up. In the deep places of the earth have they their dwelling, in the high places of the earth have they their name." Another poet, who lived nearer the sea, has left us a slightly different description of these dreaded spirits. It is as follows:

"Seven (are) they, seven (are) they!
In the abyss of the deep seven (are) they.
In the brightness of heaven seven (are) they.
In the abyss of the deep in a palace (was) their growth.
Male they (are) not, female they (are) not.
Moreover the deep (is) their pathway.
Wife they have not, child is not born to them.
Law (and) order know they not.
Prayer and supplication hear they not.
(Among) the thorns of the mountain (was) their growth.
To Hea (the god of the sea) are they hostile.
The throne-bearers of the gods (are) they.
Disturbing the *lilies* in the *torrents* are they set.
Wicked (are) they, wicked (are) they.

Seven (are) they, seven (are) they, seven twice again (are) they."

The antiquity of this poem must be very considerable, as it has been incorporated into the collection of magical texts, which, as we shall see presently, belongs to the oldest period of Accadian civilisation.

The moon-god was originally identical with Istar or "Astarte, queen of heaven, with crescent-horns," though Istar subsequently became a distinct goddess, and was identified with the planet Venus. Indeed, like the classical Aphrodite and Hekate, or Aphrodite and Artemis, Istar eventually assumed two shapes, one the goddess of love, and the other of war. The moon might be considered either as one of the bright deities who preside over love and birth, or as the queen of night and the underworld, a hostile and malignant power. In the latter form Istar was replaced by Allat, who was in the first instance merely an epithet of herself; and an old Accadian myth, the forerunner of the Greek tale of Aphrodite and Adonis, makes the infernal Allat imprison in the lower world her own double, Istar. Tammuz, the sun-god, whose name in Accadian signified "the offspring" or "only son," had been the loved one of Istar, and when the beautiful god was slain by the tusk of winter, the goddess descended into Hades, "the land from whence there is no return," to seek and find him. Dismal, indeed, was the abode of the dead, a place of darkness and squalor, where the spirits of the lost flit about like birds, with dust only for their food. Here are the phantom shapes of the heroes of antiquity, and here sit the kings, "who from days of old ruled the earth," each with his crown, each upon his throne.[1] At the gate of Hades Istar stayed awhile to demand entrance of the porter, threatening to let out the dead in the guise of vampires were it not granted her. And thereupon Allat bade the porter open and admit her, but stripped of her clothing like the other shades, "according to ancient custom." So Istar entered the land of the dead, and passed through its seven gates, leaving with the warder of each some one of her adornments—her crown, her earrings, her necklace, her mantle, her girdle of jewels, her bracelet, and her tunic—until at last stripped and bare she reached the palace of Allat, who gazed at and derided her. Then the queen of the dead ordered her satellite, the plague-demon, to smite Istar with manifold diseases, in the eyes, in the sides, in the feet, in the heart, in the head, and in all the limbs. But while the imprisoned goddess lay thus in darkness and misery, affairs in the upper world came to a standstill. The bull and the ass refused to breed, the wife deserted her husband, and the soldier would not obey the orders of his master. So the messenger of the gods hastened to the sun-god, and counsel was taken with the moon-god and Hea. And Hea created a being, called "the renewing of light," and sent it to Hades, to demand the release of Istar. When Allat heard the message, "she struck her forehead and bit her finger," and answered that she would punish the messenger with grievous pains, that its food should be the mortar of the buildings of the

[1] Compare Isa. xiv. 9, 10.

city, and its drink their offal; that the shadows of the prison should be its covering, and the battlements of the wall its habitation. Meanwhile her satellite was ordered to unveil the tablets of destiny which form the keystone of the vault of her palace, to seat the spirits of earth on their golden throne, and to give Istar to drink of the waters of life, and guide her back through the seven gates of the infernal world. At each of these she received again the ornaments she had left behind, even as the waxing moon receives once more its ornaments of light, of which it has been stripped through all the seven days of its waning quarter.

Tammuz had met his untimely death in the dark forest of Eridhu, "into the heart whereof man hath not penetrated."[1] Here was the couch of Zigara, the primæval mother of gods and men; here, too, was "the centre of the earth" and "the holy house" of the gods. By "the full waters" of a canal grew the giant "overshadowing tree," the Yggdrasil of Norse mythology, whose branches were of "lustrous crystal," extending downwards even "to the deep." Like the author of the hymn to the fire-god, the poet who has left us the shattered fragment of the story of Tammuz and the forest tree, was a native of Eridhu, a city which took its name from its bow-like shape, and lay near the mouth of the Euphrates, in southern Babylonia.

Among the other mythological poems of ancient Accad which have come down to us I will signalise one more only, although there are several others of

[1] *W. A. I.* IV., 15, 62-91.

great interest and importance for both mythology and the history of religion. The subject is one which belongs to what Prof. de Gubernatis has so happily termed "Mythical Zoology," and reminds us forcibly of the Greek myth of Tereus and Philomêla. The poem describes the transformation of the god Lugal-turda, "The valiant king," into the *Zu*-bird, a species of vulture, whose Accadian name signifies, "the bird of the divine storm-cloud." The god, we are told, "in the resolution of his heart (changed) not (his) resolution," but fled to the mountains, alone and unaided, and there found a wife in "the goddess of perfumes," "the lady of Tig-Enna." The cause of his flight is given elsewhere. The god Zu had despoiled Bel, "the father of the gods," of "the crown of his majesty, the clothing of his divinity," "the tablets of destiny," and the "secrets" of himself and the other gods. It was the theft of fire by Promêtheus over again, and in the Accadian name of the bird into which he was changed, we can trace the lightning that the god had brought from heaven to earth and thereby enabled mankind to learn the secret purposes of the deity. The Chaldean Promêtheus fled and concealed himself, after throwing all things into darkness, while the Air-god, "the mighty light," was ordered to pursue and slay him. The Air-god, however, failed in his task, and it next fell to the lot of Nebo, "the meridian sun." But Lugal-turda was immortal, and the vengeance of the gods had to be satisfied with his transformation into a bird of prey.

Such are some of the myths that were worked up into poems by the poets of Turanian Babylonia.

Their influence lasted long after the language in which they were written was extinct; they were handed on to Greeks in one direction, and Phœnicians and Hebrews in another, and so have become the heritage of all civilised mankind. Their age can only be guessed at. The Gisdhubar epic on the one side cannot be older than the formation of the Accadian calendar and zodiac, which, as it begins with the sign of Aries, must be later than 2300 B.C. On the other hand Accadian had ceased to be spoken before the 17th century B.C., and the earliest engraved gems we possess have representations taken, not only from the adventures of Gisdhubar, but from other myths as well. Perhaps, therefore, we cannot be far wrong in assigning the composition of the epic to about B.C. 2000, and referring the independent lays out of which it is composed to the centuries that immediately preceded. The bloom of Accadian poetry might then be placed just four thousand years ago, when the nature-myths, which had once expressed a very real and definite meaning, had grown faint and misunderstood, and become the subjects of numberless ballads and hymns.

But a part of the ancient Chaldean literature, which the scribes of Assur-bani-pal have preserved for us, mounts back to an older period still. Thanks to M. Lenormant's quickness of perception, we can restore from the scattered relics of a single Assyrian library the prayer books of two successive stages of religion, and of two widely different epochs of society. Behind the epical age of Babylonia lay a time which corresponded with the Vedic age of India, a time when hymns were being composed in honour of the gods, or in utterance of the spiritual yearnings of their worshippers. The hymns are all in the Accadian tongue, but they belong to a period when the Semite was already in the land, and was beginning to influence and be influenced by his more cultured neighbours. With all their civilisation, the Accadians had been Shamanistic in their religion, seeing a "spirit" in every object or force of nature, and believing that their priests, or rather sorcerers, could work good or evil by the use of magical charms. Gradually, however, all this had changed, and the time came when the higher gods were arranged in hierarchic trinities, and the multitudinous "spirits" of the earlier age were merged together among the 600 spirits of earth, and the 300 spirits of heaven. A great religious reform had taken place, a compromise between the religious conceptions of the Accadian and the Semite; the sorcerer had been succeeded by the priest, the worship of things by the worship of abstractions. It was amid the passionate movement of this religious reform that the hymns of Accad were mostly composed. Some, it is true, went back to an earlier date, and reflect, more or less faithfully, the old Shamanism of the past. But the rest are the product of the new impulse, of an age which had forgotten in part the nature-origin of the myths it was so busy in creating, and which was finding its gods in the powers of light and harmony: in the sun-god, the moon-god, and the sky. The very phrases and metaphors that are used in these old hymns are to be found in the Sanskrit hymns of the Rig-Veda, the most ancient monument of our Aryan race, and they bear witness to the fact that man has everywhere been cast in the same mould, whatever the colour of his skin or the formation of his skull, and that where the circumstances that surround him are the same, the results produced by them arc similar. Let us take, for example, a hymn addressed to the sun-god, which, while it suggests the growth of many a myth out of its misunderstood images, speaks to us in language that is not so far distant after all from that of the Hebrew Psalms.

"O Lord," the poet begins, "the illuminator of darkness, thou that openest the face (of sorrow),
Merciful god, that liftest up the fallen, that supportest the weak,
Unto thy light look the great gods,
The spirits of earth all of them bow before thy face.
The language of praise as one word thou directest,
The host of their heads bow before the light of the midday sun.
Like a wife thou submittest thyself, cheerful and kindly:
Yea, thou art their light in the vault of the far-off heaven.
Of the broad earth the banner art thou.
Men far and wide bow before thee and rejoice."[1]

Still more striking is a penitential psalm, which seems wrung from the anguish of a self-convicted conscience. The larger part of it has an Assyrian translation annexed, but I cannot do more than quote a few passages:

[1] *W. A. I.* IV., 19, 2.

"O my lord, my transgression (is) great, many (are) my sins.
O my god, my transgression (is) great, my sins (are many).
O my goddess, my transgression (is) great, my sins (are many).
O my god, that knowest (that) I knew not, my transgression (is) great, my sins (are many).
O my goddess, that knowest (that) I knew not, my transgression (is) great, my sins (are many).
The transgression (that) I committed I knew not.
The sin (that) I sinned I knew not.
The forbidden thing did I eat.
The forbidden thing did I trample upon.
My lord in the wrath of his heart has punished me.
God in the strength of his heart has overpowered me.
The goddess upon me has laid affliction and in pain has set me.
God, who knew (that) I knew not, hath caused darkness.
I lay on the ground and none seized me by the hand.
I wept, and my palms none took.
I cried aloud; there was none that would hear me.
I was in darkness and trouble; I lifted not myself up.
To my god my (distress) I referred; my prayer I addressed.

. . . . . .

How long, O my god, (shall I suffer)?

. . . . . .

The sin (that) I have sinned to blessedness turn.
The transgression I have committed let the wind carry away.
My manifold affliction like a garment destroy.
O my god, seven times seven (are my) transgressions, my transgressions are before me."

After this, it jars a little upon us to find a rubric at the end of the psalm, directing that "the name of every god be invoked sixty-five times for the tearful supplication of (the) heart," with the promise that there should be "peace (of mind) afterwards."[1]

This more spiritual class of hymns, however, is of later date than another in which the old leaven of Shamanism shows itself more or less plainly. The latter class generally introduces Merodach, the mediator and benefactor of mankind, under his Accadian name of "The Protector who does good to men," and he is required to ward off sickness and other effects of demoniacal ill-will. The hymn to the fire-god, referred to above, belongs to this class of hymns, as indeed do all those in which the seven evil spirits, the dreaded storm-clouds, are commemorated. We hear a good deal in them of charms and mystical formulæ; thus Merodach is instructed to protect the sick man from nightmare and the assaults of the seven wicked spirits, by placing a "sentence" or "verse" out "of a good book on his head while he lies in bed," as well as a wand inscribed with the name of Hea. Elsewhere the witch or sorceress is ordered to sit on the patient's bed and sprinkle him with magic water, to leave the left side free, but to bind his limbs with twice seven knots, about his head, his side, and his feet, seven being a sacred number among the Accadians as among the Jews. Such superstitions, however, were but survivals, the poems in which they are found already recognising the existence of certain supreme and omnipotent gods, and regarding the powers of evil as inferior demons, who could only work their

[1] *W. A. I.* IV., 10.

will under the friendly shelter of night. Merodach, a form of the sun-god, was especially considered the friend and helper of mankind, in whose behalf he is ever-ready to intercede with the offended deities, or to succour the sufferer in his distress. In the person of Merodach, therefore, the growing religious consciousness of Babylonia had found a mediator and redeemer, presupposing a conviction of sin. Out of this conviction arose the idea of vicarious punishment, as well as the belief in the primal purity and innocence of the human race, ruined by the successful temptation of the dragon Tihamat. A curious fragment of an old Accadian hymn describes how the sinner must give his dearest and nearest, even his offspring, for the sin of his soul, "the head of his child for his own head, the brow of his child for his own brow, the breast of his child for his own breast;"[1] and a passage in the great work on astronomy informs us, that the innocent sacrifice must be offered up by fire. The bloody sacrifices offered to Moloch, therefore, were no Semitic invention, but handed on to them with so much else by the Turanian population of Chaldea.[2]

As the Rig-Veda in India, so, too, in Babylonia, the religious hymns were collected together, and became the authorised prayer-book of the Accadian Church. But a long time must have elapsed since their composition before they could have been invested with a sacred character, and looked upon as

[1] K. 5, 139.

[2] See my Paper on "Human Sacrifice among the ancient Babylonians," in the *Trans. Soc. Bib. Arch.*, IV., 1, p. 25-31.

the authoritative text-book of the priesthood. When the civilisation of Accad passed into the hands of its Semitic conquerors, its sacred scriptures, influenced as they had been by Semitic ideas and Semitic beliefs, became the property of the new race, and the venerable ritual of both Babylonia and Assyria. As elsewhere, a superstitious reverence seems to have been attached to the mere letter and pronunciation of the sacred texts, and though in course of time a Semitic or Assyrian rendering was placed by their side, the priests had to recite them in the extinct language of ancient Accad. The Latin service of the Roman Catholic Church is the modern parallel of this curious fact, and the Aramaic paraphrases, which in later days accompanied the text of the Hebrew Bible, are not very unlike the Assyrian translations of the Accadian hymns.

But along with this authoritative canon of the priesthood went a much older collection of magic formulæ and exorcisms, which belonged to the earlier Shamanistic cult, and long remained dear to the lower classes. In these the gods of the later state religion are replaced by the spirits of heaven and earth, or else introduced fitfully and in disguise. It is difficult to know the precise place occupied by this magical collection in the reformed faith, but since the incantations are very frequently given in the Assyrian version alone, without the Accadian original, it would appear that the same respect was not paid to their mere wording as was the case with the hymns, and that the priesthood rather tolerated than approved of them. Perhaps they held a similar place to that occupied by the Lives of the Saints in the Latin Church. However that may be, the exorcisms, though going back to the most remote epoch of Chaldean history, were not all of the same date, and some even incorporate passages from the religious hymns, showing that the two periods of the magical formulæ and the hymns to some extent overlapped one another. The formulæ are almost innumerable. Nearly every event that could possibly happen was supposed to be the work of some benevolent or malignant spirit, and the formulæ were regarded as possessing power to avert an evil from oneself, or to bring it down upon one's neighbour. Thus we read: "He who makes an image to injure a man, the evil face, the evil eye, the evil mouth, the evil lips, the evil philtre—avert, O spirit of heaven; avert, O spirit of earth!" . . . . "Consumption, want of health, the evil spirit of the ulcer, spreading quinsey of the throat, the virulent ulcer, the noxious ulcer—avert, O spirit of heaven; avert, O spirit of earth!"[1] Elsewhere we are told: "Let the sorceress sit on the right and work a charm on the left; knot the knots twice seven times and wind them about the head of the sick, and about his limbs like fetters. On his bed let her sit, and the waters of magic sprinkle upon him."[2] Sometimes the formula is very explicit. Thus we are told: "Like unto this herb he is destroyed, and the spell shall burn with burning flame. To its severed stalk it shall not return; to the dish of the god or the king it shall not be brought; so shall it be with the man for whom this enchantment is

[1] *W. A. I.* II., 18, 30, etc.

[2] *W. A. I.* IV., 3, 2, 5, etc.

used. The evil invocation, the pointing of the finger, the marking, the cursing, the sinning, the sickness that is in my body, my limbs or my teeth, like this herb may it be rooted out, and on this day may the consuming fire consume. May the spell be driven out and return to its dwelling-place."[1]

It is needless to point out that this strange system of sorcery and magic survived long after the religion that succeeded it had perished and been forgotten. The "Chaldeans" of later days, who not unfrequently found a harbourage in the palaces of imperial Rome, perpetuated the sorcery and astrology of the earlier ages of Turanian Babylonia. The magic of Jews and Gnostics, of mediæval sorcerers and witches, can all be traced back to the superstitions of the primitive population of Accad. While the purer creed embodied in the religious hymns had been lost from sight and memory, the magic formulæ and beliefs of an older cult prolonged their existence almost to our own times. The human mind, untrained and uneducated, is the prey of grim superstitions; and the half-barbarous society of the middle ages was, after all, not so very unlike that of the first settlers in the plains of Chaldea. They, it is true, showed themselves capable of origination and progress, but so, too, did the society of the middle ages when awakened by the light of the Renaissance.

Like all nations who have begun to question the meaning and reason of the world around them, the early people of Babylonia were stirred by what we may term the scientific impulse. The first feeling of

[1] *W. A. I.* IV., 7, 2, 8-17.

the child is wonder at all he feels and sees, his next feeling one of curiosity to know what is its cause. As long as men are still but children, the answers they give themselves are those of children, and the growth of humanity is marked by the growing reasonableness of its interpretation of nature, and the ever-increasing accuracy of its conception of physical phænomena. The scientific impulse of ancient Accad remained an impulse only. The method of science was never discovered, the enquirer was led astray by his own fancies and misconceptions, and a pseudo-science, mixed up with numberless superstitions and false prejudices, was the result. At the same time, a systematic and persistent enquiry into the secrets of nature can never be wholly unfruitful, and amidst all the false science of primæval Chaldea there were germs of truth and brilliant discoveries which it has been reserved for our century to reveal.

The classical writers said truly that Babylonia was the birthplace of astronomy. It was also necessarily the birthplace of mathematics, and of the first regulated calendar. The Accadians had firmly grasped the principle that every effect must have a cause, though they erred in hastily assuming causes which did not exist. Their ciphers were comparatively simple, and by means of them they attained a considerable proficiency in mathematics. They made sixty their unit, and in their higher calculations reckoned it as an unexpressed multiple. Their fractions were on the duodecimal system, with a denominator of 60 always understood. The library of Larsa or Senkereh was famous for its mathematical works, and students of the science came together there for them from all sides. Some tablets from the library are now in the British Museum, and amongst these are tables of squares and cubes. It may interest our mathematicians to learn that π had been roughly valued as three, and traces of a Chaldean Euclid, with geometrical figures, have been met with.[1] It was in the service of astronomy, however, that the lives of the Accadian men of science were mainly spent. Observatories were erected in every city, and fortnightly reports were sent in to the king by the astronomers royal. The great work on astronomy, in seventy two books, to which allusion has already been made, was composed for the library of Sargon I. at Aganè, and incorporated the astronomical works and observations of preceding centuries. It was called "The Observations of Bel," the middle heaven, in which the stars were situated, being regarded as the province of Bel, and popularly known by his name. Above this central heaven came the upper sphere of Anu, and below it the terrestrial sphere of Hea. "The Observations of Bel" were translated into Greek by the historian Berosus, and enjoyed an immense reputation among the Babylonians and Assyrians. The British Museum possesses portions of several different editions of the work made for the library of Nineveh, and the original texts from which they were taken must have been greatly worn away by time and use, if we are to judge from the number of instances in which the

[1] See my Paper on "Babylonian Augury by means of Geometrical Figures." *Trans. Soc. Bib. Arch.*, Vol. IV., 2.

word "lacuna" or "obliterated"[1] occurs. The table of contents prefixed to the work, however, shows that a large part of it was purely astrological; but some of its chapters or books were of a more scientific character. Thus there was one on the conjunction of the sun and the moon; another on comets, or as they are called "stars with a corona in front and a tail behind;" a third on the movements of Venus; and a fourth on the Pole star. The work was enlarged from time to time as new observations were made; thus we have an addition to the chapter on comets, to the effect that at the time Nebuchadrezzar I. overran Elam, about B.C. 1150, "a comet arose, whose body was bright like day, while from its luminous body a tail extended like the sting of a scorpion,"[2] It moved from north to south and was accounted a presage of good fortune. As a matter of fact, more use was made of "The Observations of Bel," to discover the future, than to determine problems in astronomy. Whatever event had been observed to follow a particular astronomical phænomenon would recur, it was supposed, whenever that phænomenon should happen again. The scientific instinct was led astray by imagining that there was a connexion of cause and effect where there was simply a sequence of facts. The chapter on eclipses is especially instructive in this respect, as the eclipses recorded in it were all believed to have been the direct causes of occurrences that took place immediately afterwards; and the immense number of the eclipses shows for how great a length of time these observations must

[1] *Khibi.*

[2] *W. A. I.* III., 52, 1.

have been kept. It was part of the duty of the astronomer royal to state the event which might be expected to happen along with the record of his fortnightly observations. The Accadians had anticipated our almanack-makers in discovering a connection between the weather and the changes of the moon; indeed, all kinds of astronomical phænomena were supposed to have an influence upon the clouds; and in anticipation, as it were, of Dr. Hunter, the same weather was expected to recur after a cycle of twelve solar years. Even at this early epoch it was known that eclipses of the moon repeat themselves after a period of 223 lunations, and the records of them usually begin with the words, "According to calculation," or, "Contrary to calculation, the moon was eclipsed." As the same formulæ are sometimes employed for solar eclipses also, it would seem that the problem of calculating them by tracing the shadow as projected on a sphere had already presented itself. The problem, however, was not always successfully solved; and even as late as the seventh century B.C. we find the state astronomer of Assyria, Abil-Istar, reporting that although a watch had been kept on the 28, 29th, and 30th of Sivan, or May, for an expected eclipse of the sun, the eclipse did not take place after all, and the observers had to content themselves with a subsequent conjunction of the moon and Mercury. Even the appearance of the sun was not allowed to go unnoted, and in one place we are told, that on the 1st of Nisan it was "bright yellow," and in another that it was "spotted."[1] Who

[1] *W. A. I.* III., 62, 207, etc.

would have thought of looking for a notice of sun-spots in the clay tablets of ancient Babylonia?

The old mode of reckoning time by watches still makes its appearance in the "Observations of Bel," where the night is divided into three watches of four hours each. However, "the double hour," or *cas-bu*, as the Accadians called it, had long been in use, answering to two of our hours, and something like an accurate measurement of time was attained by the invention of the clepsydra and sundial. Indeed, however doubtful an inheritance Accad may have bequeathed to posterity in the case of astrology, it was more than compensated by its great legacy of a regulated calendar. We owe to the Accadians both the signs of the Zodiac and the days of the week. The sky was divided into four parts, and the passage of the sun through these marked the four seasons of the year, which was again divided into twelve lunar months, and 360 days. An intercalary month was added whenever a certain star, called Dilgan, or "the messenger of light," in Accadian, which was just in advance of the sun when it crossed the vernal equinox was not parallel with the moon until the 3rd of Nisan, that is, two days after the equinox. This arrangement, however, did not always suffice to keep the seasons in order; and to prevent the gods from being defrauded of their offerings, intercalary months were sometimes inserted at odd times by the priestly regulators of the calendar. The month was divided into two halves of fifteen days each, these being further subdivided into three periods of five days. But a week of seven days was also in use from the earliest ages. The days of the week were named after the sun, moon, and five planets, and our own weekdays may be traced back to the active brains of the long-forgotten people of Chaldea. The 7th, 14th, 19th, 21st, and 28th days of the month were termed "Sabbaths," or, "days of rest," when the king was forbidden to eat "cooked fruit," or "meat," to change his clothes, or wear white robes, to drive his chariot, to sit in judgment, to review his army, or even to take medicine should he feel unwell.[1] Every day of the year was under the protection of some deity or saint, and the pious believer had enough to do in carrying out the requirements of an elaborate ceremonial, and in remembering the divinities to whom he had to sacrifice his offerings, and the time of day at which he was to present them. The months were all named in Accadian after the signs of the Zodiac, the first being, in Assyrian, Nisan, our March. This was the month in which, according to the legend, Bel had offered up in sacrifice his only son, a story which reminds us perhaps of the sacrifice of Isaac, and of the ram which was substituted for him.

Fragments of planispheres show that attempts were made to map out the heavens and group the constellations together. We find from these that the equator was divided into 240 degrees; and the ecliptic, which was picturesquely called "the yoke of the sky,"[2] into 360. Lines drawn through the

[1] *W. A. I.* IV., 32, 33. See my translation of the tablet in the *Records of the Past*, Vol. VII., p. 157-168. "Medicine" is *asu*, Aramaic אסא, אסיא.

[2] *Pidnu sa same. W. A. I.* II., 47, 21.

ecliptic pole cut the equator at right angles, and formed sections distinguished by the names of their principal fixed stars. The constellations in which the fixed stars were arranged received names, many of which have lasted down to our own day. Even the milky-way was very expressively called by a name which somewhat resembles ours, *Mar-gidda*, "The Long Road." But the planets naturally claimed the first share of attention among the stars. Only five of these were known, besides the earth; and Neptune and Uranus, as well as the asteroids, had to remain unchristened until the invention of the telescope brought them within the range of human knowledge. It is not wholly improbable, however, that some kind of telescope was actually in use among the astronomers of Chaldea. One of the names given to Mars was that of "the vanishing star," in allusion to its recession from the earth; and though this does not imply more than an observation of its movements, yet when we consider that a report embodied in Sargon's collection distinctly states that Venus "rises and in its orbit duly grows in size,"[1] it would really seem that the phases of the planets had already been detected. As Mr. Layard discovered a magnifying lens of crystal at Nineveh, there is good reason for thinking that an optical instrument of some sort was not unknown. One of the tablets, relating to the motions of Venus, tells us that though it was taken from the "Observations of Bel," the original report no longer existed,[2] from which we may gather

[1] *W. A. I.* III., 57, 4, 2, and 59, 2, 13. See my translation in the *Trans. Soc. Bib Arch.*, Vol. III., i., p. 197, 218.

[2] *W. A. I.* III., 57, 4 *Rev.* 5.

some idea of the way in which this great work was compiled. There must have been many astronomical reports and other documents, however, which were not included in the collection, and among them may have been a curious Accadian table of lunar longitudes which is now in the British Museum.

While astrology was so carefully cultivated, it is not to be supposed that any means were left untried to extract predictions of the future from the events that happen on our nether earth. In fact, every event, possible or impossible, was imagined to portend some other, the nature of which had been ascertained by former experience. Sargon of Aganè was as anxious about the pseudo-science of terrestrial portents as he was about astrology, and under his direction a work on the subject was drawn up as a companion to the "Observations of Bel." There were tables of omens from births, from dreams, from observations of animals and birds, and, in short, from every conceivable accident of life, even the geometrical figures of the Chaldean Euclid being pressed into the service of the diviner. The superstitious Babylonian cannot have passed a very agreeable time. Whatever he did, said, or experienced, was fraught with the most terrible and far-reaching consequences. This pseudo-science was part of the heritage he had received from the time when Shamanism was still the religion of the country, and the change of religious opinion that had taken place meanwhile did nothing to improve his position. The place of the shaman or priest had been taken by a wrong-headed *savan*, but the *savan* had no power like the priest to avert the evil he predicted. Some of the omens are obvious enough. Thus "to dream of bright light foreboded a fire in the city," and "the sight of a decaying house" was the sign of misfortune to its inhabitant.[1] The movements of their domesticated dogs were scanned by the Babylonians with the most anxious curiosity. "If a yellow dog," we are informed, "enters a palace, exit from it will be harmful;" while on the contrary, if "a spotted dog" does the same, all things will go on prosperously. For a dog to enter a palace, however, and lie down on a chair, is a presage that the palace will be burned.[2] A long list of portents from the births of children records every accident, likely or unlikely, with the most scrupulous care. It begins in this way: "When a woman has a child and it has a lion's ears, a strong king will be in the country. If it wants the right ear, the days of the prince will be long. If it wants both ears, the enemy establish a garrison in the land and the country is reduced. If the right ear is small, the man's house will be destroyed. If both ears are small, the man's house will be built of bricks;" and so on through a long series of absurd particulars. It may, however, be interesting to know that if a child has a nose like a bird's beak, the country will suffer oppression; while if the nostrils are wanting, the country will be overrun by the enemy, and the father's house will be destroyed. But there is one occurrence which unfortunately is scarcely likely to happen, desirable as

[1] *W. A. I.* III., 52, 3, 35, 42.

[2] See my translation in *Records of the Past*, Vol. V., p. 167, et seq.

its results may be: "When a sheep bears a lion," it is said, "the troops will march multitudinously, and the king will have no rival."

It is a relief to turn from this trifling, into which the old Shamanism of the people had degenerated, to the more practical labours of the Accadians in the evolution of law and commerce. The Chaldeans were emphatically a law-fearing people, and the precedents to which their judges appealed would delight the heart of the student of Blackstone. An old table of moral precepts addressed to kings, at a time when Sippara, Nipur, and Babylon, were under one government, begins by declaring that "if the king avenges not in accordance with the law of his country, his people will perish and the country be enfeebled," while "Hea, the god of destiny," will "replace him by another ruler." On the other hand, if he turns a deaf ear to the wishes of his courtiers, and delivers judgment "according to the statutes," "the law-book," and "the writing of the god Hea," the great gods will make his throne stable and enduring. The table further informs us, that royal judges were appointed throughout the kingdom, and prisons established in the towns, and divine punishment is invoked against those who receive bribes, as well as against the officers who exact an extortionate tribute.[1] The oldest code of laws in the world is one of which only the concluding part has been preserved; but this gives the original Accadian text as well as the Assyrian translation. We learn from it

[1] Cf. my translation in *Records of the Past*, Vol. VII., 117, etc. The prison is called *bit tsibittiv*, "house of ward."

that an oath was required every day from the judges, to the effect, probably, that they would act according to justice and precedent; and that the decisions laid down in a leading case became statutable law for the future, and were ordered to be committed to memory. The state, we find, did not neglect even the slave and his children, thus asserting its rights over the property of the citizen, so far as this consisted of human chattels. "If a master," it is declared, "kills his slaves, cuts them to pieces, injures their children, drives them from the land or maims them, his hand shall measure out every day (in requital) a half-measure of corn." No doubt the punishment was slight enough, but the very fact that the slave was in any way recognised as possessing rights against his master is an important step in advance. As among other tribes of the Ural-Altaic race, descent among the Accadians was counted through the mother and not through the father, and the mother accordingly held the first rank in the family. The Accadian version of the hymn to the Seven Wicked Spirits, quoted above, declares that "female they (are) not, male they (are) not," and it is only the Assyrian rendering that reverses the order of precedence, in accordance with the Semitic view, that the woman was inferior to the man. So, too, this old table of laws is a venerable witness on behalf of "woman's rights." The son who denies his father, "confirming it by (his) nailmark (on the deed)," has only to give a pledge and a sum of silver, but a denial of the mother is followed by a severe punishment; the undutiful son has "his hair cut off, is excluded in the city from land and water, and imprisoned in the house (of correction)." The Assyrian translator felt himself compelled to soften the latter part of the sentence, and merely states that the culprit is to be "banished." It is somewhat strange that the penalty for denial of the father should be so small, since both father and mother are to be imprisoned for repudiation and neglect of their son, though it is observable that while the father is shut up "in house and brick building," the mother, as heiress and proprietor, is shut up "in house and property." Divorce on the part of the wife was nevertheless looked upon as a more heinous crime than divorce on the part of the husband, probably because it involved more serious and social consequences. The woman who offends in this way is to be thrown into the river; the man gets off with a fine of half a maneh of silver. In spite of this it is possible that some of the ladies of the present day might wish to revive the Accadian legislation of some 4000 years ago, if only for the sake of the statute which lays down that "whatever a married woman encloses, shall be her own property." The father could also put his son in possession of house property, provided he did not inhabit it; and "the chapel he erected on his high place," like the private chapels of modern bishops and noblemen, remained his own and entire possession. In accordance with a judgment delivered in a particular suit, "a chapel might be erected by the side of the high-road," which reminds us, if not of fashionable churches, at all events of the shrines so commonly met with in continental countries.[1] Church and state were intimately connected together in Babylonia, and sacrilege was accounted the worst of crimes. The authority of the judge, however, was protected by severe penalties, and fine or imprisonment awaited contempt of court.

The highroads and brickyards were placed under the care of commissioners, and the country was divided into parishes for the purpose of taxation. A bilingual catalogue of the various classes of the Babylonian population gives us some information as to the mode in which the taxes were raised.[2] The tax-gatherer was termed the "collector of the assessment" in Accadian, and the tax-payers were divided into burghers and aliens. The defaulter had a special title, and his punishment was doubtless speedy and severe. Some of the taxes were paid for the use of the public brickyards and roads, though turnpikes were probably not in existence; it is unfortunate that we do not yet know the precise way in which they were levied. At a later time, under the Second Assyrian Empire, the exchequer received a good deal from the tribute paid by subject-states. Tiglath-Pileser II. organised the districts he had conquered into satrapies, each of which had to pay a fixed sum to the Assyrian treasury every year. Separate cities, including those of Assyria itself, had also to furnish their quota towards the public expenditure. Nineveh, as the representative of Assyria, paid thirty talents, ten of which went to the general expenditure, and

[1] See my translation in *Records of the Past*, Vol. III., p. 21, et seq.

[2] *W. A. I.* II., 38, 1 *Rev.*

the remaining twenty to the maintenance of the fleet.[1] Calah paid nine talents, and Assyria, or at least that part of it in which the capital stood, was altogether assessed at 274 talents. Carchemish, long the rich capital of the Hittites, paid annually 100 talents, Arpad thirty, and Megiddo but fifteen. Besides gold and silver, the cities and provinces had also to provide chariots, dresses, and other similar contributions. Payment, it would seem, was made by weight; at all events no certain traces of a coinage have been found before the time of the Persian Darius.

In spite of the want of anything like money, however, trade transactions were carried on actively. We hear constantly in the astrological tablets of the tariff being high or low, according to the abundance or scarcity of provisions during the year; and the numerous black stones which may be seen in the British Museum, record the purchase and sale of houses, land, and other property, the most terrible curses being invoked upon the heads of all who should injure or remove these evidences of ownership. One of them informs us that the ground mentioned upon it was bestowed by the Babylonian king upon a poet-laureate, for some verses he had composed in honour of his sovereign.[2] Still more plentiful than these *stelæ*, as the Athenians termed them, are private contract-tablets, often enclosed in an outer coating of clay, on which an abstract of the contents of the inner tablet is stamped. Many of them are pierced with holes, through which strings

[1] *W. A. I.* II., 53. [2] *W. A. I.* IV., 41.

were passed attached to leaves of papyrus. The latter, however, have long since perished, like the rest of the papyri used for writing purposes by the Accadians from a remote date. Deeds of sale were frequently inscribed upon the more fragile material, and we sometimes hear of a deed of sale or an I O U subscribed by a number of witnesses. An old Accadian text speaks of an execution for an unpaid I O U, and other ancient texts record the purchase of freedom by a slave, and the pledging of a house, field, orchard, and slaves, for the interest upon a loan.[1] One of the main reasons which forced the Semitic conquerors to maintain an acquaintance with the extinct Accadian tongue, was not only that the legal formulæ and technical terms belonged to this language, but also that a large part of the property in Babylonia was held by titles which went back to Accadian times. Documents written in Accadian had constantly to be appealed to in disputes about property, and a knowledge of Accadian accordingly became as practically necessary as a knowledge of Latin in our own day.

It was the Semite, however, who showed himself then, as now, the most alive to the advantages of trade, and the fullest development of business and commerce took place among the Assyrians, who were of purer Semitic race than the mixed population of Babylonia. In the 8th and 7th centuries B.C. Nineveh was a bustling centre of trade, and its merchants had connections as far as India on the east, and possibly Tartessus on the west. The

[1] *W. A. I.* II., 13, 15-38.

commerce of Tyre and Sidon had been ruined by the Assyrian kings, acting, perhaps, in the interests of the mercantile classes of Nineveh like Edward III. in our own country; and the conquest of Carchemish, the Hittite capital, by Sargon, secured to Assyria the passage of the Euphrates, and the high road from Mesopotamia to Palestine. Carchemish, now governed by an Assyrian satrap, became a meeting-place of the merchants of all nations, and the "maneh of Carchemish" was made the standard of weight. Houses and other property were sold or leased, and the carefulness with which the deeds of sale or lease were drawn up, the details into which they went, and the number of attesting witnesses, might win the admiration even of a modern lawyer. The Aramaic of northern Syria took its place as the *lingua franca* of trade and diplomacy, and the Assyrian contract-tablets are frequently accompanied by a docket in the Aramaic language and alphabet, stating the chief contents of the documents and the names of the contracting parties. Some of the deeds are very curious. Thus we find an unfortunate girl sold by her father and brothers to Nitocris, an Egyptian lady, who wished to marry her to her son Tachos. The intended wife was only valued at about £2 8*s*., but marriage, it would seem, raised her price, as the contract could only be annulled by Nitocris or her heirs, three of whom are named, by the payment of £90. Another tablet, dated the 16th of Sivan, or May, B.C. 692, and subscribed by seven witnesses, one of them apparently a Jew, named Zedekiah, records the sale of a house "with its woodwork and doors, situated in the city of Nineveh, near the houses of Mannu-ci-akhi and Ilu-ittiya, and of the markets," to an Egyptian astronomer, who paid one maneh of silver or £9 for his purchase. The former owners of the house attached their nailmarks instead of seals to the deed, probably because they were too poor to possess seals of their own. The contract was signed in the presence of three judges. In another deed, dated the 20th of Ab, or July, B.C. 709, we have three Israelites, as M. Oppert thinks, sold by a Phœnician for £27, any retractation or annulment of the sale being subject to a penalty of £230 or thereabouts, part of which was to go to the Temple of Istar of Arbela. Some twenty years later we hear of the sale of seven slaves, among them an Israelite, Hoshea, and his two wives, for £27; the sixth witness to the sale, for some unknown reason, failed to appear and sign his name.[1]

Besides these deeds of sale, we find other documents in which silver, iron, and various objects of metal are let out at interest, the borrower binding himself to pay interest upon them in the presence of several subscribing witnesses. In one case ten shekels of the best silver are lent at four per cent. on the 3rd of Sebat, or January, B.C. 650-640, lender, borrower, and judge affixing their seals, and an Aramaic docket accompanying the deed; in another case, the 11th of Sivan, B.C. 676, two talents of iron are lent at three per cent.; and in a third case, the

[1] See M. Oppert's translations and notes in the *Records of the Past*, Vol. VII. p. 111-116.

26th of Iyyar, B.C. 667, four manehs of silver (£36) at five shekels of silver per month interest.[1] With all this interchange and reversion of property, we are not surprised to discover that something like testamentary devolution was known; and no less a document than the private will of Sennacherib is now in the British Museum. The king deposits various treasures, including gold, ivory, and precious stones, in the keeping of the priests of the Temple of Nebo, for his favourite son Essar-haddon, who at that time was not heir presumptive to the throne. No witnesses attest the will, the monarch's word and sign manual being considered sufficient.[2]

The last acquisition made by Mr. George Smith was a collection of tablets, consisting of the cheques and deeds of a great banking-firm which flourished at Babylon from the reign of Nabopolassar, the father of Nebuchadrezzar, to the end of that of Darius Hystaspis. The documents were found by some Arabs, deposited in a number of earthenware jars, which served the purpose of our modern "safes." The founder of the firm was a man named Egibi whose descendants carried on the business through five successive generations. The father regularly took the son into partnership with himself, as soon as he arrived at years of discretion, and only retired from business when age or health seemed to require it. The firm now and then lent money to the kings of Babylonia or Persia, like the Rothschilds of a later date, and the extent and continuance of its

[1] See my translations in *Records of the Past*, Vol. I., p. 139, et seq.

[2] *W. A. I.* III., 16, 3.

commercial transactions, in spite of the capture of Babylon and the overthrow of the Babylonian Empire, is evidenced not only by the number of deeds, but still more by their regular succession. Among the deeds is the banking calendar, in which the bank-holidays are scrupulously recorded, and the days are noted as "lucky" or "unlucky," "days of humiliation,"[1] and the like.

The commercial spirit of the Semitic race could not, however, wholly extinguish the love of agriculture which the climate and soil of Babylonia had implanted in the hearts of its inhabitants. The Accadian reading-book compiled for educational use by the Assyrians, contained a good number of passages from a work on agriculture, which seems to have resembled in some measure "The Works and Days" of Hesiod, or the book of farming maxims of early Rome.[2] The farmers' year was divided into three seasons, and quite a large assortment of agricultural tools was employed by them. One of the maxims of the old farmers' guide instructed them to "plough, break up, and harrow their fields at the time of sowing,"[3] which was usually in the month Adar, or February, and the canals and other works of irrigation throughout the country were carefully looked after and provided for. Market-gardeners might lease the ground of richer proprietors, and in one place we read that of the whole produce the

[1] *Yumi biciti*, literally "days of weeping."

[2] See Festus, *Ep. v. Flaminius*, p. 93; Macrob., *Sat.* V., 20; Serv. *in. Georg.*, I., 101; Pliny, *N. H.*, 17, 2, 14.

[3] *W. A. I.* II., 14, 17-20.

tenant should "measure out two-thirds of the vegetables for himself and (leave) the rest for the owner of the garden."[1] The garden was sometimes called the orchard, and most houses possessed one. The weeds and waste produce of the ground were burned in the most approved fashion. Oxen were employed for farming purposes, horses, "the animals from the east" as the Accadians called them, being reserved for war and hunting; and the farmer's guide-book contains some short songs with which the Accadian ox-drivers beguiled their labours in the field. "Before the oxen as they march, all in the grain thou layest thee down," is one; "The knees are marching, the feet are not resting; thou hast nought of thine own, so serve me with thy labour"[2] is another. In a third we read, "Heifer that thou art, be yoked to the cow; the plough's handle is strong; the share cuts deep,[3] lift it up, lift it up!" from which we may see that the Accadians did not object to put the cow to other than milking uses, like some of our continental neighbours.

I will not weary your patience with any further details respecting the old literature which is being recovered from the mounds and buried cities of Assyria and Babylonia. If complete it would form an encyclopædia of the arts and sciences of greater extent and more worthy of study than the famous *Origines* of S. Isidore of Seville. The inner and outer life of the primæval Chaldeans, whose cry was in their ships, and whose walls were adorned with

[1] *W. A. I.* II., 15, 43-47. [2] *W. A. I.* II., 16, 28-33.

[3] Literally, "is bowed" or "bent." *W. A. I.* II., 16, 34-38.

figures in vermillion, is brought before us in all its minuteness and manifold activity. We can watch the changing currents of their thoughts, can map out their knowledge, and gauge their intellectual strength. The civilisation which existed on the banks of the Euphrates more than 4000 years ago almost startles us by the modernness of many of its details. The literature it has left is of large and varied extent, the work of many minds and many centuries. There is much in it, it is true, that sounds strange and *bizarre* to our unaccustomed ears, and it will never hold the same place in our memories and affections as that occupied by the literatures of Palestine, of Greece, and of Rome. But for all that it is well worthy of study, and even if we judge it from a merely literary point of view we shall find much to admire. The bald and literal translations of the modern scholar can give no idea of the force and beauty of many of the poetical compositions; it needs the rhythmical language and hallowed associations of the authorised version of the Old Testament to make us feel how closely the hymns and legends of Accad resemble the writings of Hebrew priests and prophets, in both language and imaginative power. But it will be long before the Assyrian student can venture to give them the English garb that best befits them; and longer still, perhaps, before he can fill up the numerous gaps and lacunæ which mar the effect of the finest passages. Apart from their literary value, however, the records of ancient Babylonia are inestimably precious for the study of language, of history, and of religion. The culture and traditions of the Accadian were inherited by the Semite, and through the Semite have become the possession of Greeks, of Romans, and of the modern world. Much that hitherto seemed inexplicable in mythology and religion is now having a flood of light cast upon it; customs, ceremonies, and beliefs, whose very origin has been a mystery, are now being cleared up and explained. We have reached the source of the civilisation of Western Asia, we have found its primal fountain; and the nature and geography, so to speak, of this source and fountain are being disclosed to us in all their fulness and all their outlines. The primitive Chaldeans were pre-eminently a literary people, and it is by their literary relics, by the scattered contents of their libraries, that we can know and judge them. As befitted the inventors of a system of writing, like the Chinese they set the highest value on education, even though examinations may have been unknown among them. Education, however, was widely diffused; I have already drawn your attention to the fact that Assur-bani-pal's library was open to the use and enjoyment of all his subjects, and the syllabaries, grammars, lexicons, and reading-books that it contained, show the extent to which not only their own language was studied by the Assyrians, but the dead language of ancient Accad as well. It became as fashionable to compose in this extinct tongue as it is now-a-days to display one's proficiency in Latin prose, and "dog-Accadian" was perpetrated with as little remorse as "dog-Latin" at the present time. One of the Babylonian cylinders found by General di Cesnola in the temple-treasure of Kurium, which probably belongs to the period of Nebuchadrezzar's dynasty, has a legend which endeavours to imitate the inscriptions of the early Accadian princes; but the very first word, by an unhappy error, betrays the insufficient knowledge of the old language possessed by its composer. Besides a knowledge of Accadian, the educated Assyrian was required to have also a knowledge of Aramaic, which had now become the *lingua franca* of trade and diplomacy; and we find the Rab-shakeh (*Rab-sakki*), or prime minister, who was sent against Hezekiah by Sennacherib, acquainted with Hebrew as well. The grammatical and lexical works in the library of Nineveh are especially interesting, as being the earliest attempts of the kind of which we know, and it is curious to find the Hamiltonian method of learning languages forestalled by the scribes of Assur-bani-pal. In this case, as in all others, the first enquiries into the nature of speech, and the first grammars and dictionaries, were due to the necessity of comparing two languages together; it was the Accadian which forced the Semitic Assyrian or Babylonian to study his own tongue. And already in these first efforts the main principles of Semitic grammar are laid down clearly and definitely; the Assyrian grammarians at any rate had small doubt of the triliteralism of Semitic roots. It is significant that the Assyrian legend of the Creation, a legend which must be subsequent to the time when a philosophising spirit had resolved the old gods of the people into manifestations of a single deity and elaborated a syncretic cosmogony, begins with the assertion, that, "At that time the heaven above was unnamed, in the earth beneath a name was unrecorded." Still more significant is the commencement of the far older legend of the Creation from Cuthah, which tells us, that, "On a stele one wrote not, one disclosed not, and the bodies and produce from the earth he caused not to come forth."[1] Chaos was conceived of as a period when there was no literature, and the distinguishing feature of the monstrous and Titanic races that preceded humanity was their ignorance of books and education. The primitive Chaldean had grasped the fact, that without literature there can be no history. We learn from classical writers that Babylonia once possessed Universities, and we may infer from the native literature that has come down to us that it also possessed schools. The day may yet come when we shall find records and details of these schools, and the education they afforded; at present we can only infer that they were to be found in at least every great city, and provided instruction in reading, writing, and ciphering, to say nothing of instruction in that dead language which was to the Babylonian what Latin is to us. The public libraries, founded and fostered by kings and princes, were open to all, and the mass of literature they contained, as well as their varied contents, show pretty plainly how large must have been the literary class of the country, and the readers of its productions. Where clay was the chief writing material, the multiplication of books was easy and inexpensive, and the publisher

[1] *Ina D. P. narā ul isdhar ul iptā'-va pagri u sebatti ina mati ul yusetsi.*

was quite unneeded. Hence we can readily understand the existence of this China of Western Asia, a nation at once learned and well-educated, among whom, it may be, discussions on the merits of school-boards had already been heard, and provision been made for lectures to ladies. "There is nothing new under the sun" is an utterance, the truth of which is daily being impressed upon us by the discoveries in Babylonia or Egypt; ours is not the first age of civilisation the world has seen, and many "modern improvements" may yet turn out to be but revivals of what was known and practised on the banks of the Tigris and Euphrates some forty centuries ago.

APPENDIX.

Page 6, line 21.—Dr. F. Delitzsch has recently suggested that Accad and Sumir were not respectively south-eastern and north-western Babylonia, as has hitherto been believed by Assyrian scholars, but that the converse was the case. Two facts, however, go to show that the ordinary opinion is correct. First of all, Sumir, or Sungir, answers to the Hebrew Shinar, Accadian (*n*)*g* (for original *m*) between two vowels being represented by Hebrew ע(נ), as in Cudur-lagamar = כדר־לעמר, or Turgal = Θοργὰλ, תרעל, and since Shinar contained the cities of Babel, or Babylon, Erech (now *Warka*), and Calneh, or Kul-unu, it must have been in the north-west. In the second place, a syllabary gives Uri, or Ur, the modern Mugheir, as the Accadian equivalent of [cuneiform], "Accad," and Ur falls within the southern division of the country.

Page 7, line 22.—For the tradition that the Phœnicians had originally come from the Persian Gulf, see Strabo i. 2, 35; xvi. 3, 4; 4, 27; Justin, xviii. 3, 2; Pliny, *N. H.*, iv. 36; Herodotus i. 1; vii. 89; Schol. to Homer, *Od.*, iv. 84.

Page 8, line 31. For these tables of squares and cubes see my paper on "Babylonian Augury by means of Geometrical Figures" in the *Trans. Soc. Bib. Arch.*, Vol. IV., 2, p. 311-314. The tables belong to the Accadian epoch, the square being called *ibdi*, and the cube *badie*.

PAGE 9, line 24.—The Assyrian text (though unfortunately mutilated) is as follows (*W. A. I.* III., 52, 3 *Rev.*, 33):

. . . . *ina*	*dippi-ca*	*mi-nav*	*ta-gab-bi*
. . . . on	thy tablet	the number (which)	thou statest

i-gab-bu-ca-va ci . . . .
(the librarian) shall state to thee and according to . . .

PAGE 11, line 14.—The cylinder from Kuruim runs thus:

1 *Abil-D.P.-Istar*
Abil-Istar

2 *abil Ilu-ba-lid*
son of Ilu-balid

3 *ebed D.P. Na-ra-am-D.P.*-EN-ZU.
servant of the god Naram-Sin.

PAGE 11, line 18.—The analogy of other Kossæan names compels us to read the final character in the name of Khammuragas as *gas*, not *bi*, and to analyse the name into Khammu-ragas, "the god Khammu begets." *Ragas* would be connected with the Accadian *răcci*, "a woman." The insertion, therefore, of 𒄿, *i*, after the royal name Agu-ragas (written *A-gu-um-ra-gas-i*) in S. 27. 2. 19, must be due to a blunder of the later Assyrian scribe who misread the final characters. Such mistakes are to be found elsewhere.

PAGE 11, line 26.—The text of the fragment is given in *W. A. I.* III., 64. The colophon states:

1 *Duppu I.* *'Sinu* *tamarti-su*
The first tablet (beginning) "The Moon (at) its appearance
sāpā . . . . .
whiteness . . . . .

2 *cī pī* *D.P. li-khu-ši* *duppi* *gab-ri*
According to the papyrus of the tablet in parallel

Babili
columns of Babylon.

3 *D.P. D.P. Nabiu-zu-ku-up-cinu abil D.P. D.P.*
Nebo-zukup-cinu the son of
Maruduc-mu-ba-sa D.P. a-ba
Merodach-mubasa the astronomer

4 *a-na ta-mar-(ti)-su va si-ta-as̍-s̍i-su*
for the inspection of himself and his people

5 *a-na tsa-mar(a) ina nalbar-same ip-tal-lim*(?)
at the rising on the horizon has copied (them)(?)

PAGE 14, line 7.—*Ni-s̍ic duppu-sadh-ru*, "the engraved characters of the tablets." *Nis̍ic* is found in many passages followed by *abni*, "stones," or *abni sudhurruti*, "inscribed stones" (*W. A. I.* I., 53, 2, 30, etc.). The verb *esci*, "I carved," occurs in *W. A. I.* II., 66, 2, 6. *Kips̍an s̍um-ci*, "the literature of the library," the first word being the construct plural, and the second word connected with the Accadian *s̍umuk* and *s̍amak*, "a library." *'Sumuk* is rendered by the Assyrian *sūtu*, and *s̍amak* by *mutstsatu*, the compound ideograph representing the latter being literally "a collection of tablets." (See the Syllabary, Nos. 175 and 176, in my *Elementary Assyrian Grammar.*)

PAGE 14, line 21.—For the statement as to the position occupied by the hymns, see K 48, where it is said that "9 hymns" (*telilāti* = KHIR-KHIR), were "on the west side of the library," the first being addressed to Asshur, while "on the east side" were "15 hymns in all," the second of which was addressed to Bel-makhira, "Bel the confronter."

PAGE 17, line 22.—The inscription of Rimmon-nirari I. is dated in the eponymy of Sallim-ma-nukaradu; that of Tiglath-Pileser I. in the eponymy of Ina-ili-ya-allac.

Page 19, line 3.—The spelling-lesson will be found in *W. A. I.* III., 16, 2.

1 *A-bat* *binat* *śarri* *a-na*
The prayer of the daughter of the king to

2 *nesat* *D.P.* *Assuri* *sar-rat(i)*
the lady of the city of Asshur the queen:

3 *a-ta-a* *um-pi-ci* *la ta-sadh-dhi-ri*
why *umpici* dost thou not write?

4 *im-pu-ci* *la ta-gab-bi-i*
impuci dost thou not say?

5 *'u-la-a* *i-gab-bi-u*
thus they say.

6 *ma-a* *an-ni-tu-u* *belat-śa*
This (is) the prayer to her lady

7 *sa* *D.P.* *D.P. Serua-e-dhe-rat*
of Serua-edherat

8 *binati rabi-tav* *sa* *bit ridā-te*
eldest daughter of the harem

9 *sa* *D.P.* *Assur-ebil-ili-yuc-in-ni*
of Assur-ebil-ili-yucin,

10 *śarru rabu* *śarru dan-nu* *śar cissati*
the great king, the strong king, king of multitudes,
sar mat Assuri.
king of Assyria.

11 *va* *at-ti* *ma-rat dan-nat* *bilati* *sa*
and thou (art) the potent lady, the mistress of
D.P. Assur-bani-pal
Sardanapalus

12 *abil* *śarri rabi* *sa* *bit ridā-te*
son of the great king of the harem

13 *sa* *D.P. Assur-akhi-iddina* *śar* *D.P. Assur*
of Essar-haddon king of Assyria.

Page 20, line 1.—The tablets relating to the invasion of Assyria by the Medes and their northern allies are unfortunately very much mutilated. They are, moreover, merely the rough copies of the scribe, the capture of Nineveh having, perhaps, prevented fair copies from being taken, and the characters are therefore exceptionally hard to read. So far as the texts are at all perfect, they run thus, S 2005:

1 [*D.P. Samsu bilu*] *rab-u sa a-sal-lu-ca*
O Sungod, lord great, whom I will call to thee
il simti cini a-pal [*an-ni-nu*]
O god of fixed destiny, remove our sin.

2 [*D.P. ca-as*]*-ta-ri-ti bil eri sa D.P. Car-cas-si-i*
Castarit lord of the city of Car-cassi
sa a-na D.P. ma-mi-ti-ar-su
who to Mamiti-arŝu

3 [*bil eri*] *sa nis ma-da-ai is-pu-ru um-ma*
lord of the city of the Medes had sent thus:
*it-ti a-kha-*I *nis-sa-cin it-ti*
"With one another we are established with
mat . . . .
the country of . . . . (we are confederate)."

4 [*D.P. ma-mi*]*-ti-ar-su i-sim-me su-u* SEMU*-su-u*,
Mamiti-arsu hears: he his hearing
pa-ni-su i-sac-[*can*]
before him makes

5 . . . . SA*-an-na an-ni-ti it-ti D.P. D.P. As-sur-*
this year with Assur-
akhi-iddi-na sar [*mat Assuri ta-kha-za i-sac-can*]
akh-iddina king of Assyria war he makes

6 . . . . *ci-i ilu-ut-ca rabu-ti* . . . .
. . . . according to thy great divinity . . . .

7 . . . . *ra sa D.P. Ma-mit-ar-su bil eri sa*
. . . . of Mamiti-arsu lord of the city of
nis ma-da-[*ai*] . . . .
the Medes . . . .

8 . . . . . [*D.P. Assur-akhi-iddi-na*] *šar mat Assuri-ci*
. . . . Assur-akhi-iddina king of Assyria
i-na . . . .
in . . . .

The rest of this tablet is too broken to be legible, but mention is made of the "city *'Sa-an-du-li-tir*," and of the *nis 'Sa-par-da-ai*, or "people of Sepharad," on the coasts of the Black Sea (see Obad. 20). K 4668:

1 *D.P. Samsu bilu rabu u-sa-al-lu-ca il*
O Sun-god, great lord, I have asked thee; O god
simti cini apal an-ni-[*nu*]
of fixed destiny remove our sin.

2 *istu yumi carari yumi III. sa arkhi an-ni-i*
From the current day, the 3rd day of this month,
arkhi GUT-'SI-DI *adi yumi XV. sa arkhi*
the month Iyyar, to the 15th day of the month
NE *sa sanni carari*
Ab. of the current year,

3 *a-na C yumi C musi carari me-sa-ri*
for 100 days (and) 100 nights current, sacred rites
i-šin-ni D.P. khal-ti i-na
(and) festivals let the commander-in-chief among
si-da-ri . . . .
the ranks [proclaim]

4 *lu-u D.P. ca-as-ta-ri-ti a-di tsabi-su lu-u*
since Castarit with his soldiers, since
tsabi D.P. gi-mir-ra-ai
the soldiers of the Kimmerians,

5 *lu-u tsabi D.P. ma-da-ai lu-u tsabi*
since the soldiers of the Medes, since the soldiers
D.P. man-na-ai lu-u nacari cal-sunu
of the Minnians, since the enemy, all of them,

6 *i-zar-ri-mu i-cab-bu-du . . . . lu-u ina*
inundate (and) are multitudinous . . . . since on
si-bu-u-tu lu-u . . . .
the seventh (day) then . . . .

7 *lu-u i-na i-śin(i) tiglat kabli u*
then during the festival by means of conflict and
takhazi . . . . lu-u bi-lis-si GIS-KAN *ippalcut-u*
battle . . . . then ? ? have revolted
napalcuti
the revolters.

8 *lu-u i-na dir-ra-pa-khi-ma lu-u . . . . lu-u*
Then with warlike engines(?), then . . . . then
i-na bu-bu-ti
with famine

9 *lu-u ina a-di-e u se-mu ili u . . . .*
then with an oath and obedience to god and (king)
lu-u i-na mukh-khi ic-ma-si . . . .
then with in addition ? . . . .

10 *lu-u i-na rac-śa si-par-ti . . . . . âli*
then with the bond of a letter . . . . . the cities,
cal-sunu
all of them,

11 *D.P. ći-sa-aś-su-tai . . . . lib-bi D.P.*
the city of the Cisassutians . . . . the midst of the city
khar-tam D.P. ci-sa-aś-śa il-mu-u
Khartam, the city Cisassu they approached;

12 *D.P. khartam D.P. ci-sa-aś-śu katā-śu-un*
the city Khartam, the city Cisassu their hands
i-cas-sa-a-da
captured.

13 *a-na ka-ti-su-un im-ma-ni-i D.P. Samsu*
to their hands numbered (them) the Sun-god,
inu rabu-ti . . . .
the mighty eye (together with)

14 *V. . . . . D.P. khartam D.P. ci-sa-aś-śi*
5 (villages of) the city Khartam (and) the city Cisassu
i-na katā nacari cal-sunu
in the hands of the enemy, all of them.

15 *istu yumi carar-i adi yum si-ci-ri i-na*
From the current day to the day of the feast in
irtsi-tim i-na pan ilu-ti-ca rabu-ti
the land in the presence of thy great divinity

16 *e-zib . . . . lib-bi-su-un i-dib-bu-bu i-turu-*
I left . . . . the midst of them they plot; they return
va . . . .
and . . . .

The next 8 lines are too mutilated for transcription: then comes

26 *ci-i sa yumi carar-i yumi III. sa arkhi*
Since that the current day, the 3rd day of the month
. . . . GUT *adi yumi XI. sa arkhi* NE
Iyyar to the 11th day of the month Ab
sa sanni carar-ti
of the current year

27 *lu-u D.P. ca-as-ta-ri-ti adi tsabi-su nis tsabi*
then Castarit with his soldiers (and) the forces
nis gi-mir-ra-ai lu-u tsabi nis man-na-ai
of the Kimmerians, then the forces of the Minnians,

28 *lu-u tsabi nis ma-da-ai [lu-u] nacari*
then the forces of the Medes, then the enemy,
cal-sunu
all of them,

29 *D.P. khar-tam D.P. ci-sa-as-sa . . . . .*
the city of Khartam, the city of Cisassu (they approached),
D.P. khar-tam D.P. ci-sa-as-ṡu-tai
the city of Khartam, the city of the Cisasṡutians

30 *D.P. khartam D.P. ci-sa-aṡ-ṡa katā-sun*
the city Khartam the city of Cisassa their hands
i-cas-sa-du a-na ka-ti-su-un im-man-du-u
captured; to their hands they were measured.

Mr. Boscawen has recently found a fragment of another tablet relating to the same events, in which Castarit is called "king of the Medes."

PAGE 29, line 17.—*Alala*, "the eagle," seems but another form of *Tammuz*, "the sun-god," since the Accadian *alala* is given by the side of *alam* as an equivalent of *tsalamu*, the mighty "image" of *Samsu*, "the sun." In the syncretic age of Assyrian theology Alala was resolved into a form of the supreme god Anu (see *W. A. I.* I., 54, 3, 11 and 4, 42).

Page 29, line 29.—For Datilla, the river of death, see *W. A. I.* II., 62, 2, 50.

Page 30, line 14.—*Tutu* is explained by *erib-samsi* on an unpublished tablet, and he sometimes appears as *Tu*, or "sunset," (scc for example, *W. A. I.* III., 67, 21, where *Tu* is called the god of "death"). *Tutu* is addressed as *mu'allid ili*, *muddis ili*, "the generator of the gods, the renewer of the gods," in K 2107, and in *W. A. I.* III., 53, 2, 15, as "he that prophecies in the presence of the king."

Page 32, line 14.—Hence the Accadian name of the month Tisri, "the month of the holy mound."

Page 35, line 4.—See Dr. Delitzsch in the Appendix to the German translation of Smith's *Chaldean Genesis*, p. 308. He points out that the *yumi muttakputuv*, or "revolving days," answer to the Syro-Palestinian "seven *mustakridhât*," which intervened between the 25th of February and the 3rd of March, and whose dangerous character became proverbial.

Page 36, line 24.—The Accadian original, in accordance with the respect paid to women in Accad, where the mother was the head of the family, has the reverse order: "female they are not, male they are not."

Page 40, line 17.—*Dup simti*, or "tablets of destiny," is plain enough, but my translation of *tereti* as "secrets" is given very doubtfully. The Sun-god is called "the lord of *tereti*" (e.g., Lay. 87, 9), and I am inclined to connect the word with *eru* (הרה), "to conceive." The two lines in the tablet before us (K 3454), col. ii., 12, 13, are (12) *lul-ci-va dup simti ili a-na-cu* (13) *vâ te-ri-e-ti sa ili ca-li-su-nu lu-akh-mu-um.*

PAGE 54, line 19.—In S 1907, we have an Accadian text which tells us: . . . *mul mulene agu lal* MU-*bi gina-ta* "(when) the star of stars is parallel with the moon, that year is normal;" . . . UTU III. *mul mulene Agu lal* MU-*bi dirru*, "(when after) three days the star of stars is parallel with the moon, that year is wanting." In the colophon of the tablet given in *W. A. I.* III., 53, 1, reference is made to the appearance of Dilgan, or *Icu* as the Assyrians called it, in the month Nisan, at the beginning of the year.

PAGE 55, line 18.—The first month of the year, corresponding with Aries, was called by the Accadians *itu zag-garra*, "the month of *zag-garra*," which is interpreted "the god Bel" in *W. A. I.* II., 47, 48, and *asib paracci asirtuv*, "the frequenter of the altars of righteousness" in *W. A. I.* II., 35, 55. The Phœnician legend of the sacrifice of Yeoud (Yekhad ?) by El will readily be remembered.

PAGE 55, line 26.—See the fragment of an astrolabe, marked S 162.

PAGE 57, line 5.—I have given a translation of this table of lunar longitudes, which is written in Accadian, in *Nature*, Oct. 7, 1875. DU = "it advances," MI-NI = "it retrogrades," literally "it becomes obscure."

PAGE 60, line 1.—The oath of the judges is alluded to in the colophon of the Law Tablet

(*W. A. I.* II., 10, 23). The Assyrian translation of the first words of the following tablet run *mala urri mamitu*, "every day, an oath."

PAGE 62, line 10.—The bilingual text in *W. A. I.* II., 38, 1 *Rev.*, deserves careful study. First of all we have the "tax-gatherer," *da-lu-u* (דלה) *sa bil-ti*, CI-TA being all that is left of the Accadian equivalent. Then *ra-pi-ku*, "the assessor" (Aram. רבק), in Accadian LUGUR AL GAR-A, "the man who makes assessment." Then *khi-bu-u*, "the defaulter" (חבא), Accadian LUGUR GAR-ŚUN GAR-A, "the man who makes default." Then *má-ci-śu*, "the collector" (مكس), Accadian LUGUR GAR-TAR-DA GAR-A, "the man who makes judgment." Then *la-bi-in li-bit-ti*, "the brickyard overseer," Accadian LUGUR *ucu* ZI-TAKH, "the man who superintends the bricks." Then *la-kidh kur-ba-an-ni*, "the collector (לקט) of the taxes" (קרבן), Accadian LUGUR *lak* RIRIGA, "the man who collects the assessment." After that *a-si-bu*, "the squatter," or "alien," Accadian LUGUR CA-CA-MA, "the man told over," and *ca-tu-u*, "the burgher," Accadian LUGUR CA GINA, "the man of the fixed face." The Accadian words are all written ideographically, and their pronunciation is therefore uncertain, the two in italics alone excepted.

PAGE 69, line 16.—The Assyrian text of the latter part of the third ox-driver's song is unfortunately lost, but the whole of the Accadian original has been preserved. It runs thus:—

1 *D.P.* *va-a-na* *me-en*
A heifer am I (= Ass. *a-ga-la-cu.* Heb. עגל.)

2 *D.P.* *mul-cu* *ab-lal-e*
the cow-to one yokes (= Ass. *ana pa-ri-e tsa-an-da-[at]*, "thou art yoked," permansive, Heb. צמד.)

3 *gis-gar* *su-gi* *me-na-nam*
the plough the handle is strong (Ass. *nar-cab-ta*, "the plough," רכב.)

4 GI *u-ki*
the share cuts deep

5 *ab-ili* *ili-e-en*
lift it up lift (it) up.

For *su-gi* see *W. A. I.* II., 27, 43, where *su-gi* = *ma-kha-ru sa rucubi*, "the front part of the chariot." For *na-nam* (= *ci-nu*) see *W. A. I.* II., 1, 38; III., 70, 10.

www.ingramcontent.com/pod-product-compliance
Lightning Source LLC
LaVergne TN
LVHW020653100826
845148LV00012B/2465

* 9 7 8 1 6 0 6 0 8 8 2 7 2 *